VENTURES OF FAITH

The Story of Mennonite Biblical Seminary

Samuel Floyd Pannabecker

**Mennonite Biblical Seminary
Elkhart, Indiana
1975**

CONTENTS

FOREWORD

"Venture of Faith" is what some of the supporters called the 1958 relocation of Mennonite Biblical Seminary from Woodlawn Avenue in Chicago to Benham Avenue in Elkhart. Others had less approving ways of describing the event. In retrospect, the story of ministerial training in the General Conference Mennonite Church is a series of ventures of faith. Each step, whether it resulted in brief institutional life or a longer one, was undertaken in earnest response to what was understood to be the leading of God in a way to meet a felt need for better qualified congregational and conference servants and leaders.

Samuel Floyd Pannabecker, superbly competent for the task, was commissioned by the administration of Mennonite Biblical Seminary to research and write up this story. Not only was Pannabecker considered qualified for this task by reason of his training as an historian but also because he has written the most comprehensive comtemporary interpretation of the development of the General Conference Mennonite Church which sponsors Mennonite Biblical Seminary, and he has personally been involved in strategic leadership positions in the seminary since 1947. His meticulous patterns of record keeping, his keen perception of historical process, his avocational skills in photography, and his delightful sense of humor all contribute to his skill as a reporter. His professional standards of fairness and objectivity and his own modesty are readily perceived in the product. No one, thus far, really knows the whole story of Mennonite Biblical Seminary in its historical context and its contemporary expression better than the author. Before its

5

publication, however, the manuscript was also read by a number of colleagues including Paul Mininger who was president of Goshen College and Goshen College Biblical Seminary at the time of the negotiations which led to the formation of the Associated Mennonite Biblical Seminaries. This book is published in recognition of the 30th Anniversary of Mennonite Biblical Seminary with special endorsement of the MBS Alumni Association. For the several hundred former students and graduates of the seminary, this story will help to recall many former experiences. For others, this brief account carefully researched and documented, will serve as an aid to understanding one of the cooperating schools in the Associated Mennonite Biblical Seminaries program. It is hoped that all who read it may perceive here a witness to God's gracious working through the power of His Holy Spirit.

Grateful recognition is here also given to Rachel Hilty Friesen (Class of 1973) who edited the manuscript and to Mary Troyer who typed it for publication.

Erland Waltner, President
Mennonite Biblical Seminary

January 15, 1975

1

MENNONITE MINISTERIAL TRAINING BEFORE 1900

Traditional Patterns

Reformation times of the sixteenth century saw three prime patterns in the work of the ministry. In the inherited system of the Catholic Church, the minister was primarily a **priest,** gathering candidates, young and old, en masse into the fold of the church by the rite of baptism and shepherding them by other **sacramental processes** into mature Christians. The grace of God, of which these rites were the outward manifestation, worked through repentance, baptism, penance, and especially the Eucharist to accomplish this transformation.

It was against the misuse of the outward aspects and the accumulated powers of the priesthood that the Reformers protested, leading to their final break with the church. All of these — Luther, Calvin, Zwingli — turned to the Bible for authority and attempted to bring a true conviction and repentance by **preaching of the Word.** The sacraments were retained as valid but robbed of their mystery, while the minister was primarily a **preacher** leading the people into the Kingdom of God through instruction.

The Anabaptist forerunners of the Mennonites, as the third party, followed the Reformers in emphasis on the Bible but parted with them when they adopted the state church pattern and baptized converts en masse. The early Bible study groups popular in Reformation churches were retained by the Anabaptists long after these groups lost popularity in the large churches. Leaders in these small devotional groups were not preachers, much less dispensers of the sacraments. They were simply devoted members, counselors, chosen or accepted for their piety and zeal. They encouraged and exhorted the little flock to earnestness and often pledged with their own lives their faithfulness.

From this simple type of leader developed the Mennonite ministry. To his duties as counselor was added that of preaching the Word, while another representative of the congregation was chosen to supervise the acceptance of candidates and perform the rites of baptism and communion which were retained as symbols rather than sacramental means of grace.

By 1700 when the first heavy immigration of Mennonites to America began, the Mennonite ministry had crystallized into a three-fold ministry: the deacon, who assisted in material and spiritual care of the congregation; the preacher of the Word; and the bishop or elder who had overall supervision. Each was selected as needed from the congregation, required no special training, and served devotedly with no thought of remuneration. This was the form of ministry which had spread throughout Europe and which also was brought to America — a most effective system for days of persecution or migration.

The eighteenth century, however, was to see changes in the European church and consequently in its ministry. Holland, where the Mennonites were early granted freedom, felt the moves first. City congregations chose men with formal education, often professional or business men, as ministers, and gave them modest financial assistance for time lost in their business. Then was introduced private training of young men by older experienced ministers and finally in 1735 an institution was opened with one professor and six students. The type of minister thus changed from the early exhorter to the educated minister and even to the university-trained theologian.[1]

In North Germany, where the Mennonite stock was Dutch and long influenced by Dutch language and customs, churches often sent young men to Holland for training and

1. For interesting articles on this transformation see, *Menn. Blaetter* XXXIII, 26ff (April, 1886); XXXVIII, 18ff (Feb. to April issues, 1891); and for South Germany, ibid., XXIX, 60ff (Aug. and Sept. 1882).

followed Dutch patterns until the language changed and created a more distinct barrier. In South Germany, where the background was Swiss, the northern influence was slower in making itself felt, but by 1800 marked changes were occurring. There was relaxing of the earlier strict rules; there were marriages outside the congregation and meeting houses were being built. Ministers were reading sermons; youth were getting more education. The Weierhof school was opened with higher education in 1867.

First General Conference Ministerial Training

It was from this South German situation — through recent immigrants to America — that the stimulus for the organization of the General Conference Mennonite Church came. Of the key men, Daniel Krehbiel, arriving in 1832, was one of the first. An active layman, he proposed the 1859 meeting which effected union of the Iowa churches and urged further action. Daniel Hege, teacher from the Palatinate who arrived in 1851, ardently advocated union and proposed a seminary. Youngest of the group was Christian Krehbiel, not yet thirty, who arrived from the Weierhof in 1851, attended the 1859 meeting, and was prominent in all General Conference sessions after 1863.

To these new immigrants should be added the names of three native-born American Mennonites: John H. Oberholtzer, older and active, who had long favored union but so far in vain; Andrew B. Shelly and Ephraim Hunsberger, younger but active in the later sixties in the Conference and the school.

The first project to which these men and their newly organized Conference turned their energy was a ministerial training institute. In the second Conference session, held in 1861, Daniel Hege called for men not only to know the power of the gospel but to be able to transmit it effectively. Out of this came the proposal and plan for a **Christliche Bildungs-Anstalt der Mennoniten Gemeinschaft.** Later located at Wadsworth, Ohio, it became popularly known as the Wadsworth Institute. A building was erected in 1865 and dedicated in 1866, although there was no faculty at hand. Carl Justus van der Smissen, a university-educated North German pastor, was called to teach and

9

arrived in 1868. In the meantime, with Christian Schowalter in charge, the school had already opened in January 1868.

The Institute was an heroic undertaking. The school records show 209 students identified by name and place of origin during the first nine years, or until the end of the 1875-76 school year.[1] With the following year the Institute was divided into two separately directed schools — a theological school in the German language and a normal school in English. The number of students in the German department decreased rapidly and discouragement mounted, with closing at the end of the eleventh year. The Institute's path was never smooth, though sometimes promising. The end came in 1878 due to mounting debts, inner discord, disagreement between eastern and western congregations over its purpose, and finally lack of students.

The Wadsworth effort has been lamented as a "failure." Its closing was unfortunate. In addition to the school difficulties, other interests interfered. The Russian Mennonite immigration, under way in the seventies, and the attention to foreign missions drew the attention of the Conference and diverted financial resources. But the school was not a complete failure. New students attended every year. The largest student body, new and old, numbered forty-four in 1873-74. Among the 200 plus students all areas of the General Conference were represented. The largest number naturally was from Ohio, almost ninety in all. The majority of these were Wadsworth local students, but there were also fifteen from the nearby Swiss community and ten from the farther Butler County Amish group. Pennsylvania provided over forty students; Illinois sent about twenty, while Indiana and Missouri Swiss sent another dozen. Even Europe had a half dozen students over the years at Wadsworth. For a decade this intermingling of young men inoculated their congregations with new ideas about church work — missions, evangelism, Sunday School, temperance, and the ministry.

The Wadsworth Institute introduced a new concept of

---

1. The original Wadsworth school record books are in the Bethel College Historical Library, a microfilm copy at Mennonite Biblical Seminary, and other historical libraries.

the ministry — trained men, open to a call from other congregations than their own, with visions of new possibilities. They spread across the whole Conference area. Some returned to their home congregations, e.g., S. F. Sprunger to Indiana, J. S. Moyer, A. M. Fretz, N. B. Grubb to Pennsylvania, and P. P. Lehman to Missouri. Others crossed the country to new locations: Manasses S. Moyer of Pennsylvania to Oklahoma; John S. Hirschler from Summerfield, Illinois, to Hillsboro, Kansas; Isaac A. Sommer from Dalton, Ohio, to Berne, Indiana; and J. B. Baer from Summerfield, Illinois, to Bluffton, Ohio, to serve as Conference evangelist. Not to be forgotten are S. S. Haury and H. R. Voth, pioneer missionaries to the American Indians.

Wherever these men went, there was a quickening of church life and conversely, wherever there was new life, there were likely Wadsworth influences at work. For the churches that were then members of the General Conference, the Wadsworth Institute, for better or for worse, signaled the end of the old lay ministry and traditional forms of church life.

Wadsworth Institute came to an end, but its spirit and its work were continued in a series of district institutions established for much the same purpose. Russian Mennonites in Kansas opened the Halstead **Fortbildungsschule** while the ashes of Wadsworth were still warm. It grew into Bethel College. In the Middle District came Central Mennonite College and about the same time, Freeman College in the Northern District. All aimed at the promotion of church life and preparation of an adequate ministry. The next attempt at training for a ministerial career was to be of somewhat different character.

The Interim Period (1878-1915)

Forty years elapsed between the close of the Wadsworth school and the next attempt at formal ministerial training. In the meantime the effects of Wadsworth and its immediate successors were being felt. The *Mennonite Yearbook* records the obituaries of eighty ministers who died in the years between 1896 and 1940. They represent the ministers from the nineteenth century who were trained in the old ways and were first to break away from the old patterns.

11

The changes came slowly but are quite obvious. Some interesting observations can be made.

The ministers can be divided into three groups, distinguished by growing differences: (1) those who died before 1909 and served mainly from 1860 to 1900 (2) those who died between 1910 and 1925 and served mainly from 1890 to 1920 (3) those who died after 1925 and served mainly from 1910 to 1935-40.

In all groups the men were largely foreign born; of the eighty obituaries from 1890 to 1940, only twenty-eight referred to American-born men. Of the foreign born, about one-third were South German-Swiss and two-thirds North German-Russian. The arrival of foreign-born ministers for U.S. congregations ceased about 1890, but their services continued long after.

The large majority of these eighty ministers, fifty-six to be exact, were called by their home congregations and served one congregation only. Those who served other congregations than their own were very few at first but the number increased as time went on. Of the first group of fifteen, only one left his home. He was Manasses S. Moyer, a Wadsworth student from Pennsylvania, who made contact with the Swiss churches and was drawn into their orbit.

Of the second group, eight left home to serve other congregations, and of the third group of thirty-five, sixteen relocated away from home. In all cases it was almost entirely the school-trained men who served other than their own congregations.

The conclusion here is obvious: Ministerial training and mobility go together. Wadsworth, Halstead, and later the colleges pioneered in producing a new type of minister, available and welcomed where need arose. With mobility came also other changes — active promotion of missions, Sunday Schools, evening meetings, and evangelism. Along with these might be added Christmas trees, freer use of music, store-bought clothing, and even watch chains. All such things became more common as time passed.

After 1900, increasing vacancies in pulpits and a growing foreign mission work fostered the sentiment for a new institution which eventually blossomed as the first attempt at an American Mennonite graduate theological seminary.

2

GRADUATE MINISTERIAL TRAINING INTRODUCED

The time was now 1912. Fifty years had passed since the Wadsworth school had been proposed and over thirty since it had closed. Times had changed. The industrial revolution was well under way; the automobile was appearing and was about to break the transportation barrier. The First World War was to come shortly, but no one on this side of the Atlantic knew it. In fact, it was an age glowing with promises of peace and good will. A Federal Council of Churches had been organized with proposals of united church action on morals and social problems. The General Conference had joined the Council in 1908, though it was to withdraw after ten years. High school and even college education was growing more common among Mennonite young people. Mission fields had been opened and were calling for youth. The Mennonite colleges which up to this time had been little more than academies of high school grade had new blood in their administrations and were aspiring to become standard colleges and grant bachelor degrees.

As to the ministry, men of the Wadsworth generation were still active, along with those of the traditional type, but were being supplemented by a few men with college and seminary training. These men started in the pastoral ministry, but most of them were drawn into educational work — J. H. Langenwalter and J. W. Kliewer to Bethel College, N. C. Hirschy and S. K. Mosiman to Bluffton College. It was from those of this college background that the initiative for the next ministerial training institution appeared. It was really part of a broader impulsive move toward a united Mennonite educational institution, a move no doubt valid but probably premature.

There were in 1912 three Mennonite colleges struggling to attain status but all having difficulties — Bethel, Bluffton, and Goshen. N. E. Byers, president of Goshen College, had suggested the possibility of a united Mennonite college. J. E. Hartzler, newly appointed dean, proposed a graduate seminary, but both he and the president felt the time was hardly ripe for the step unless a broader foundation could be found. One step led to another until the presidents of the three colleges met for a consultation in December 1912. A further step in May 1913, brought together twenty-four representatives of five Mennonite groups who approved the idea of a joint venture in a standard college and theological seminary.[1] This was the move that resulted in the transformation of the small academy and junior college of the Middle District (Central Mennonite College) into Bluffton College and Mennonite Seminary. It should be understood that the representatives of the five groups were not officially appointed, nor did the action involve church approval. Further, any existing Mennonite college might have been the base of the new effort, but for various reasons the lot fell to the Bluffton school, infusing new life and hope into that institution. A full story of these moves may be found in the *Story of Bluffton College*.

Witmarsum Theological Seminary

The Middle District of the General Conference continued its support of the reorganized college as did the Eastern District and the Central Conference which later merged with the General Conference. None of the other bodies gave official or financial support to the move except that the Mennonite Brethren in Christ elected board members for several years and encouraged a few students to attend. Thus the aim of a cooperative endeavor was not fully realized. Valuable assistance from Mennonite sources came when the reorganized college opened with N. E. Byers and

1. The five Mennonite groups which had members participating in the discussions and early organization were: The General Conference, the Mennonites (MC), the Mennonite Brethren in Christ, the Defenseless Mennonites, and the Central Conference of Mennonites.

C. Henry Smith on the faculty. Both transferred from Goshen College, Byers to be dean and Smith professor of history.

Mennonite Seminary thus began in 1914 as a department of Bluffton College, along with the college of liberal arts and a school of music. The tie-in with the college had certain advantages, but there was a growing feeling that the seminary could develop better and serve a wider constituency as an independent institution. Thus in 1921 the Bluffton College Board of Trustees agreed to turn over certain assets to a new seminary board elected from various branches of the Mennonite church. The reorganized seminary, now called Witmarsum Theological Seminary, continued the previous work without interruption beginning in the fall of 1921. J. E. Hartzler, formerly dean and president of Goshen College but at that time serving as president of Bethel College, accepted the position of president of the new seminary. P. E. Whitmer became dean. Mennonite Seminary and Witmarsum Seminary accordingly can be regarded as one continuous operation under two different names.

Obvious differences between this ministerial training effort and that of Wadsworth are the higher level of education pursued and the fact that a full complement of American-trained teachers could be found. Another difference is that Wadsworth was a move sponsored by the whole General Conference, while Witmarsum was administered by an independent board, self-perpetuating in fact, though actively supported by certain district conferences. Both had to go out and win their way financially, and both had to sell themselves to the church at large. Both also ended after a period of less than two decades, Witmarsum in 1931.

Witmarsum's best days were the mid-twenties, about 1924 to 1928. The accommodations were modest, but acceptable. The building assigned to the seminary by the college had originally been a two-story, four-bedroom residence. It had earlier served the college as a women's dormitory and after Witmarsum closed, it reverted to the college and was used as a music hall. In Witmarsum's use, the first floor kitchen became the library with about 1000 volumes initially. By the end of the decade, the number had been doubled, and under the care of Dean Whitmer the

Witmarsum Students of 1926-27

back row	middle row	front row
Delbert E. Welty	Emil A. Sommer	Wilmer S. Shelly
T. A. Van der Smissen	Martha Graber Landis	Clara A. Willier
John L. Davidson	Harold H. Eyman	Jerry Sauder
Alfred Habegger	Eva G. Harshbarger	Lena Waltner
Raymond Hilty	Oscar L. Holmes	Earl L. Salzman
	Clyde W. Black	Eunice N. King
		W. Harley King

books were well chosen. The former dining room became a classroom, and the parlor doubled as classroom and chapel. In this fashion the old square frame building became the symbol of Witmarsum Theological Seminary. In its halls there were stimulating intellectual activity and a fervent spirit.

Three men constituted the core of the faculty in the early years: J. H. Langenwalter as Dean served in theology, P. E. Whitmer in Bible and church history, and J. A. Huffman in New Testament and Greek. All taught college courses while college men supplemented in certain fields — N. E. Byers in religious education and C. Henry Smith in Mennonite History. Upper class college students mingled with seminary students in many courses. With reorganization a clearer distinction became evident between college and seminary faculty and students. Whitmer was the only one of the earlier three to continue, but he served loyally through all the years from 1916 to 1931 and was Dean to the Witmarsum arrangement. J. E. Hartzler came on the scene in 1921 and A. E. Kreider first taught in 1923. These three were the long-time core of the Witmarsum faculty. Two others each served for three years (1922-1925), namely, H. A. Fast and Jacob Quiring. Several college teachers again assisted in the fields of public speaking, sociology, and music, while A. S. Rosenberger taught part-time in Greek and college Bible courses.

The faculty was a creditable group and commanded the respect of students, college, and community. Courses were planned in three areas, or departments as they were called: one for college graduates, leading to the degrees of A.M., Th.M., or B.D.; one for high school graduates, called a theological college course, with a Th.B. degree; and one for students with a limited education, in Bible studies with a diploma on completion. These were supplemented by a half dozen courses offered on a correspondence basis. The number of students undertaking correspondence work was few and demand for Bible school courses decreased until their discontinuance was recommended by the Dean in 1929. While the levels of study were distinguished carefully, students mingled freely and constituted a single body.

The number of students in attendance varied. For three of the years it was very low — two, four, and six respectively for the first and last years of Mennonite Seminary and the last year of Witmarsum. Otherwise the average was sixteen or seventeen. The following table will give a detailed summary.

TABLE OF
STUDENT ATTENDANCE AT WITMARSUM THEOLOGICAL SEMINARY

	Mennonite Seminary							Witmarsum Theological Seminary										
School Year	1914-1915	15-16	16-17	17-18	18-19	19-20	20-21	21-22	22-23	23-24	24-25	25-26	26-27	27-28	28-29	29-30	30-31
GC Students Men	1	8	7	8	9	4		13	10	9	4	2	9	11	7	3	
Women			1		1				1	2	3	4	4	7	3	3	
GC Total	1	8	8	8	10	4		13	11	11	7	6	13	18	10	6	0
Other Menn.	0	5	4	9	3	0		5	8	4	6	2	1	0	2	1	0
Non-Menn.	1	1	1	1	2			2	1		1	4	2	8	12	14	6
Total	2	14	13	18	15	4		20	20	15	14	12	16	26	24	21	6

The actual number of persons registered in the Seminary over the years from 1915 to 1931 was 140. Twenty-six of these attended in the earlier period and 114 in the Witmarsum years. Of the total, ten were registered as correspondence or short-term students, twenty-eight were part-time students only, and 102 were regular full-time students. Of the overall total, General Conference students numbered eighty, other Mennonites twenty-eight and non-Mennonite thirty-two. All districts of the General Conference were represented in the student body: Eastern ten, Middle twenty, Central thirteen, Western twenty-seven, Northern eight, and Pacific two. Students from east of the Mississippi numbered somewhat more in the early years, but those from the West increased in number and accounted for a few more than half at Witmarsum. The years from 1926 to 1929 are characterized by the presence of a number of missionaries who spent furlough time in seminary studies.

By 1930 fifty-three persons had been graduated from the various courses with thirty receiving the B.D. degree, ten the Th.B. degree, and thirteen the Master's degree. Over forty were in active church service as of that date, twenty-three in the pastoral ministry, eleven as foreign missionaries, and seven as teachers. The *Witmarsum Bulletin* commented on the number of graduates "all rendering some service to our Mennonite churches." The Dean credited this to Witmarsum's love for the church and the spirit of respect for her past and hope for the future which it inculcated in students. He insisted that the Mennonite church must have its own seminary if young people were to be retained for the church.[1]

Financially the Seminary had both good news and bad news. The bad news was that the institution was always in straitened circumstances. After the organizational meeting of the new Witmarsum board, there were no funds to pay traveling expenses of the board members. Faculty salaries were always low, student aid funds were insufficient or nonexistent, and library purchases were limited. The good news was that the institution was able to keep out of debt to the end. During the first summer of Witmarsum organization, it was possible to go out and solicit cash and

1. *WTS Bulletin,* Vol. V, No. 2, June, 1926, p. 1.

pledges to the amount of $20,000. In 1922 the Eastern District took official action to support one chair by the amount of $2,000. The Middle District and Central Conference followed suit. Soon after, the three districts in the West also pledged support. Thus the Seminary had official backing and modest support.

Building and equipment were sufficient in the beginning to satisfy the immediate simple needs of a small school, but there were aspirations for something more elaborate and impressive. "Students," the Dean's report said in 1926, "are tremendously influenced by brick and mortar in choosing a school." The Seminary became more conscious of needs in comparison with other schools, especially when Kelley's *Theological Education in America* appeared in 1925. It was a study which for the first time attempted to evaluate ministerial training in America. Witmarsum participated in the study and joined the association which was later to become the American Association of Theological Schools (now the Association of Theological Schools) and the accrediting agency for seminaries. Witmarsum administrators recognized the good assets they had in faculty, loyal students, and substantial supporters but stressed for creditable operation, new housing, endowment, library, and dependable income. These they felt could be realized if the Seminary were given a reasonable chance to present its case to the churches.

As early as 1924, the President presented to the Board the need for long-range planning. The Board appointed a Committee on Future Planning which reported in the following years. The Dean presented three reports in successive years, 1925 to 1927: "A Standard Theological Seminary," "An Efficient Seminary," and finally, "A Ten-Year Project." Yet the needed action did not materialize.

The year 1926 seems to have marked a critical time. The President pointed out three periods in the life of the school: (1) 1913-21, when it was part of Bluffton College (2) 1921-26, when it was independent but on the Bluffton campus (3) from 1927 on should be a period of expansion to inaugurate a program which could command respect for the next 50 to 100 years. For this program there were three possibilities as to permanent location. Bluffton was one possibility, a large city or university campus was another, while the third was affiliation with some older recognized theological seminary. The President recommended the third choice. These possibilities were discussed pro and con but never was a final decision made.

Delay in making a decision as to permanent location was due to several factors, but probably the financial situation was the greatest of these. In the early twenties Bluffton College was entering an active endowment solicitation program. Witmarsum officials hesitated to compete with the college and postponed action until the college might be successful. Five years was the estimate. They waited twice five years for the successful culmination only to have the depression wipe out the supposed gains. At the end President Hartzler felt the Seminary had lost its opportunity. "Patience tires in time," he said. His own inclination ever since taking up the presidency had been for eventual affiliation with some larger institution. With Board approval he had corresponded with several — Bonebrake, now United Theological Seminary in Dayton, Hartford in Connecticut, New York Biblical, and Bethany in Chicago. Finally it was 1930, and no permanent program was yet in sight for the Seminary.

It was under these discouraging circumstances that the President resigned and the school closed at the end of the 1930-31 school year. To the unsolved location problem was added the decrease in the number of students and especially of Mennonite students in the last few years. This, however, was probably but another aspect of the deteriorating situation and not a final cause. Under better circumstances the work probably could have continued on the Bluffton campus and a proper program found in time, but the Board seemed to feel that a temporary closing would allow for clearing the air and enable a renewed attempt in a few years. No one anticipated a closing of more than five years at the most.

One cannot leave Witmarsum with the thought of a run-down institution perishing through neglect. It was rather a living, throbbing experience for most of those who participated in it. The list of students and graduates contains the names of dozens of men and women, some active even forty years after Witmarsum closed. Who can forget such pastors as Elmer Basinger, first B.D. graduate in

1917, or A. J. Neuenschwander, the second B.D. man in 1918? Their successors were men such as G. T. Soldner, 1920; H. A. Fast, J. M. Regier and P. K. Regier, all B.D., 1922; A. S. Rosenberger, B.D., 1923; W. S. Shelly, B.D., 1927. Missionaries attended, some on furlough, some before going to the field. Their names are equally well known — Aganetha Fast, Th.B., 1926; Elizabeth Goertz, Th.B., 1929; Samuel T. Moyer, B.D., 1928. Others attended without finishing a degree, e.g., W. C. Voth and S. J. Goering. They cannot all be named but the General Conference would not be what it is without them.

No one who was there at the time can forget Martha Graber Landes who attended Witmarsum from 1925 to 1928. Born in Switzerland, she sought U.S. citizenship but was twice turned down in court at Lima, Ohio, due to her pacifist principles. She was finally successful. Nor can a fellow student forget LeRoy Mitchell, black Baptist minister from Lima, with a booming voice and hearty greeting. He persisted in studies year after year until granted a B.D. in 1923, and an A.M. in 1926. Other non-Mennonite B.D. graduates added luster to the student body: Clyde Black, B.D., 1929, Methodist; Maurice Kidwell, B.D., 1929, of the Church of God; Franklin R. Mason, B.D., 1930, Presbyterian; and finally from the last year Marion E. Tinsler, Methodist minister, a loyal supporter of Witmarsum who went on for further studies and served as Dean at Ohio Northern University.

From other Mennonite groups came men who later made their mark in their churches: John H. Lohrentz, Mennonite Brethren missionary to India and later President of Tabor College; Harry F. Weber, from the Mennonite Church (MC) of Illinois and author of a book with that title; Jerry Sauder of the Evangelical Mennonite Church, Indiana. There were also over a dozen who received a Master of Arts degree from Bluffton College for work done in the Seminary. Some went on to validate the shaky degree by further postgraduate study but always regarded the Witmarsum work as significant.

So Witmarsum came and went but left a legacy of devoted workers for the church and introduced graduate ministerial training. Thereafter that was the training sought. Other institutions then welcomed Mennonite students and other denominations often profited by their services.

3

MENNONITE BIBLICAL SEMINARY, CHICAGO

Another Interim (1931-1945)

The year or two of closing that the Witmarsum Board anticipated lengthened out to fourteen years. Yet this period was not without activity. The Board met annually to look after endowment investments and real estate mortgages, concluding this period with $11,000 in liquid assets. Reminders of the former work and continuing needs were regularly published in conference reports and in such special accounts as that of P. E. Whitmer in the October 25, 1938, issue of the *Mennonite*. Whitmer pointed out that twenty-five of the men and women graduates of Witmarsum were serving in important capacities in Conference work. They were joined by an additional number of men who had attended seminaries of other denominations.

The interim gave opportunity to test out Conference opinion on Seminary training. Although there remained a place for Bible schools on a different level and for Bible departments in the colleges, there was a strong feeling that graduate training of a more professional nature was the preferred preparation for the ministry. There was discussion, especially on the idea of affiliation with another institution, and various suggestions were made.

In preparation for the reopening of Witmarsum there were three matters that demanded attention: (1) the reorganization of the Board and administration to effect a closer tie to the General Conference and the Mennonite Church as a whole (2) the selection of a head for the institution, and (3) the decision in regard to location and program of the revived institution. These three questions were discussed repeatedly throughout the interim years. Solution of the first matter was completed by 1940, but the others remained unresolved until 1945.

Reorganization of the Board

The reorganization of the seminary board was suggested soon after the closing of Witmarsum, and a special committee was appointed to propose a plan. The report of the committee, under I. R. Detweiler, was thoroughly discussed and approved at a special meeting of the Board on April 21, 1936. The new plan provided for direct election of seminary board members by the constituents. The General Conference was to have six representatives, the Central Conference three representatives and any other conference wishing to cooperate also three representatives. The alumni were allowed two representatives on the board and the Mennonite colleges each one representative. To this new board, when organized, would be transferred all assets of the Seminary, and the Witmarsum graduates would be asked to consider themselves as alumni of the new institution.

The difference between this and the previous board is obvious. That board was essentially an independent, self-perpetuating body. The original members in 1921 were selected by the Board of Trustees of Bluffton College to represent the six Mennonite bodies involved in the Bluffton College board. Thus the Seminary Board had members from the General Conference Mennonite Church, the Central Conference Mennonites, the Mennonite Church (MC), the Mennonite Brethren in Christ, the Defenseless Mennonite Church, and the Mennonite Brethren. Each Mennonite body was to elect its own representatives "provided said branches of the church desire to do so."[1] In case the group concerned failed to elect representatives, the seminary Board was empowered to do so. Actually only the General Conference and the Central Conference made a pretense of electing members; the Board then ratified these and chose

1. WTS Constitution, 1921, Art. V, Sect. 2.

others as suitable. The same was true when alumni members were added to the Board.

The new plan thus provided for a Board authorized by and responsible to the Church. It also assumed eventual control by the Church with a sense of responsibility for financial support. This plan was referred to the Education Committee of the General Conference and with recommendations by them to the Session of the General Conference in 1938, when, with some modification, it was approved. The modifications provided that the college and alumni representatives should be advisory members without vote and that, until the seminary reopened, special efforts should be made to reinforce the college Bible departments.

The reorganization meeting of the Seminary Board took place on February 13, 1940. The list of members of the "Old" Board and the "New" Board gives evidence of the continuity of the program.

"Old" Board Members		"New" Board Members	
Allen Yoder	Central Conference	Allen Yoder	Central Conference
I. R. Detweiler	Central Conference	I. R. Detweiler	Central Conference
Emanuel Troyer	Central Conference	Emanuel Troyer	Central Conference
E. G. Kaufman	General Conference	E. G. Kaufman	General Conference
P. E. Whitmer	General Conference	P. E. Whitmer	General Conference
J. E. Amstutz	General Conference		
		Lester Hostetler	General Conference
		E. W. Baumgartner	General Conference
		A. S. Rosenberger	General Conference
		C. E. Krehbiel	General Conference
L. L. Ramseyer	Bluffton College	L. L. Ramseyer	Bluffton College
		P. K. Regier	Bethel College
		J. D. Unruh	Freeman College
H. T. Unruh	Alumni	H. T. Unruh	Alumni
W. S. Shelly	Alumni	W. S. Shelly	Alumni

All members of the "Old" Board carried over to the "New" Board with but one exception, viz., J. E. Amstutz. He, along with Yoder and Troyer of the Central Conference, had served continuously on the Witmarsum Board from the beginning in 1921. I. R. Detweiler, E. G. Kaufman, and Lester Hostetler all had also had several years of experience on the "Old" Board before serving on the "New," as had the Alumni representatives. The "New" Board consequently was but a slight modification of the "Old" with the addition of new General Conference members. It may be noted that with the "New" Board a number of persons became members who were to continue for long terms of responsible service. A. S. Rosenberger was to be President of the Board for almost twenty years; E. W. Baumgartner was to be Treasurer for over twenty-five years. R. L. Hartzler soon replaced Troyer on the Board and then served as Secretary for fifteen years. J. N. Smucker, A. E. Kreider, and Willard Claassen, all elected a few years later, each contributed fifteen or more years.

In this fashion a Board of Trustees was set up and the reorganization procedure approved by the 1941 session of the General Conference, as well as by the Central Conference in official session. The new organization was still called the Board of Trustees of Witmarsum Theological Seminary and was ready as of 1941 to tackle the two outstanding problems of seminary leadership and location.

Leadership and Location of the Seminary

While reorganization of the Board could be discussed apart from other problems, the two questions of leadership for the proposed new institution and its location and program could not be separated. The story of the search for a leader is a tantalizing one. As early as 1933, futile attempts were made to find someone to undertake the position without specifying exactly what his work would be. Under discussion at the same time was the question of plan and program but ideas were still indefinite. A special committee had worked in 1930 on the matter of affiliation with other seminaries, of which Bethany Biblical Seminary in Chicago seemed to have some preference. During 1932-33 Dean Whitmer carried this further by outlining with Bethany a possible program whereby each institution would have independent organization with its own faculty members contributed to the joint operation and its own enrolment of students. Other details regarding courses, credits, graduation and similar questions were also spelled out. The proposed program received favorable consideration by Bethany and the possibility of further positive steps seemed likely.

The Bethany proposal received a serious setback in 1935 when a special session of the Middle District Conference was called and, led by the more conservative members, registered strong opposition to a seminary not organized on fundamental principles of faith. This criticism was directed at Bethany. The charges were later softened and rebutted but never entirely eliminated. In view of this kind of criticism both Witmarsum at an earlier date and the new board in 1940 felt it wise to make a clear statement of faith to apply to the institution. The Board statement in behalf of Witmarsum had been made back in 1924, when they affirmed that:

> The Scriptures of the Old and the New Testament are the inspired work of God which holy men of God spake as they were moved by the Holy Ghost. [1]

Apart from this they expressed accord with the historic and well-known Apostles' Creed. The new board's statement was that which was cleared by the Conference session in 1941, commonly known as the Souderton Statement.

The new Board of 1940 resumed discussion of plans for reopening the seminary and seemed again favorable to the Bethany affiliation. A special committee had reported this as the most desirable plan though they suggested as an alternative an independent institution on or nearby one of the college campuses. The time was judged as inauspicious and no action taken. The question arose each succeeding year, however, and could not be sidetracked. In 1941 the whole Board, with one exception, concurred in pursuing the program with Bethany. Here the plan without the leader was incomplete, and a unanimous call was given to E. G. Kaufman, then President of Bethel College, to head the new seminary attempt. Kaufman, a member of the Seminary Board, was sympathetic to the proposal but felt unable to leave his college position. Among other attempts was a call to Dr. M. C. Lehman, recently returned from MCC relief work. Lehman tentatively accepted but withdrew when he found that the institution he was to head would not be accredited. In 1943, S. F. Pannabecker was

---

1. Minutes of the Annual Meeting of the Board of Trustees of WTS, Feb. 5, 1924 Official Record Book, p. 46.

approached but when he was not released by the Mission Board under which he served, he returned to China for relief work. Nevertheless, the Board agreed to open in affiliation with Bethany in the fall of 1944, "or as soon thereafter as possible," and made one more attempt by inviting H. A. Fast to the head position. He again "did not see the light" to accept.

The repeated frustration was somewhat discouraging, but the plan received stimulus by an energetic proposal from E. G. Kaufman in June of 1945. Kaufman first wrote to the officers of the Boards, A. S. Rosenberger, President, and J. N. Smucker, Vice-President, under date of June 20, and then on July 2, to the members of the Special Committee on Plans and Program of which he was a member. Rosenberger's response illustrates his own mood of frustration and that of some members of the Board and underlines the venturesomeness of the proposal. Kaufman's proposal was, in effect, that the seminary be opened in September of that same year in affiliation with Bethany. Rosenberger, appalled, replied that after seeking repeatedly for four years in vain to accomplish this very thing, the Board would be expected to do in four weeks what had not been possible in four years. By what magic would it be possible to find four people willing to move to Chicago and serve on a seminary staff, to make living arrangements in the city, to contact Bethany and work out the details of an affiliated program, and to secure the approval of the related boards, then to induce students whose plans had already been made to transfer to a new untried program? It did seem somewhat preposterous but, looking back, perhaps it was the Holy Spirit rather than magic which actually accomplished all of that.

The proposal was well thought out and presented to the Board through the Special Committee on Plans and Program at a meeting on July 31, 1945. It was based on the assumption that this was an opportune time. The War in Europe was over. Several college graduates of that spring were known to be looking for a suitable school; a number of young ministers were seeing a place for additional training; and men in Civilian Public Service were being released and were ready for study. The Conference had given the Seminary a green light and would be expecting some kind of action. Certainly, the Committee felt, a minimum of one or two suitable leaders could be found.

The Special Committee consisted of A. S. Rosenberger, J. N. Smucker, L. L. Ramseyer, and E. G. Kaufman. Kaufman, on instruction from the Committee, had traveled to interview possible faculty candidates and had found at least six men who would be willing to teach part-time during the next two years. This meant that at least one man could be present each term representing the Mennonite faculty participation. Conference response seemed enthusiastic. Dr. Rufus Bowman, President of Bethany, was encouraging the move. More particularly there was a candidate for the Seminary head — Abraham Warkentin. Warkentin, who was living in Chicago at the time, was then engaged in visiting C.P.S. camps, and Kaufman had interviewed him out in Downey, Idaho. Warkentin's response was favorable and assumed that release from his C.P.S. visitation program would be feasible. With this preparation the Board met on July 31, 1945.

This Board meeting was one of the most strategic in the history of the Seminary. The sessions were opened and closed with prayer and with a sense of the vital significance of the occasion. There was long and serious discussion, yet the results can be reported rather briefly. In essence the recommendations of the Special Committee were adopted. Affiliation with Bethany Biblical Seminary was approved; Abraham Warkentin was elected President for the coming year; and the institution name was changed from Witmarsum Theological Seminary to Mennonite Biblical Seminary. A part-time faculty of not less than three was to serve each year; a scholarship of $150 was to be made available for each full-time student; and a budget of $10,000 was approved for the first year. Further action was taken authorizing a call to J. M. Regier to serve as Field Secretary, and appointing an Administrative Committee of four — A. S. Rosenberger, J. N. Smucker, E. G. Kaufman, and L. L. Ramseyer — to assist the President in details of coordination, personnel, publicity, and such matters.

Opening of Mennonite Biblical Seminary

The interval from the Board meeting on July 31 to the opening of the Seminary school year on September 4 was a busy time. Dr. Warkentin returned to Chicago immediately and became involved with correspondence regarding faculty and students, with the preparation of a catalog and other publicity, and with negotiations with the Bethany staff. The Administrative Committee, especially the college presidents, joined him in working with prospective students. A list of some thirty students known to be concerned about seminary training was prepared and individual letters sent to them. Some expressed interest in an interview and in visiting the place. Accordingly a meeting was arranged on August 31, and all prospects invited to attend at Seminary expense with no obligation to enrol. September 4 arrived and with it the opening of school and the enrolment of fifteen students: ten in the graduate Seminary, two in the Bible School, and three in the Home Study Department. Mennonite Biblical Seminary had materialized.

Whether the institution so established merited the name of seminary or not is beside the point. It was given that name — The Mennonite Biblical Seminary and the Mennonite Bible School. Before many years passed the Bible School had few students and was discontinued, while the seminary eventually became an independent accredited theological school. The beginning was very modest, though the aspirations were great. The opening was celebrated in a formal service on October 4, 1945, in the Bethany chapel with a welcome address by Rufus D. Bowman and responses and addresses from the Mennonite representatives. The dedicatory sermon by A. S. Rosenberger was based on Psalm 127:1, "Except the Lord build the house, they labor in vain that build it." He emphasized that we must be **God-minded** — feel the call of God; that **God's book** be given a central place — the Indispensable book; that we **preach the gospel** of Jesus Christ — the way to real peace; and that the institution be accredited by **service rendered for God** by its graduates and students. He closed with a quotation from one of the Board members:

Because we do not have the institution to start with that we had hoped, because it is not as complete and with the faculty we had hoped to have . . . perhaps that will make us look to God the more.

So, he concluded, we look to God, and we hope to grow.[1]

The dedicatory prayer by J. N. Smucker may long apply to the school there founded and is worth recording here.

O God, our help in ages past, our hope for years to come, it is with deep gratitude in our hearts that we pause in this quiet moment to give Thee thanks for all Thou hast done for us, for all the blessings that have come from Thee that we can now come to this moment, to the formal opening of the school. Our Father, we would consecrate and dedicate unto Thee the institution, the plans, the prayers that have gone up in its behalf and will continue to ascend unto Thee. We would dedicate the students, the teachers, and all those responsible for this institution. We would dedicate to Thee our young men and young women, that they here may find Thee face to face and go forth in Thy name, preaching the gospel. We would dedicate to Thee all the future that lies before us. The work is Thine, O Lord, not ours. We would be but channels through which Thou canst work and obtain Thy ends. We would dedicate our resources, our prayers, our concerns, and our labors unto Thee in behalf of this Thy institution. God grant that as these sister institutions work together, they might all be found closer to Thee and to each other. This we pray in the name of Christ our Lord as we dedicate ourselves unto Thee and unto this Thy work. Amen.[2]

The First Two Years

At the Seminary Board meeting held the afternoon of the same day, President Warkentin reported on progress and plans for the year. The Bethany Board had met and formally approved the affiliation. Part-time teachers had been secured for the year, each to serve for one term: C. Henry Smith, Mennonite History, in September and October; C. E. Krehbiel, Mennonite Polity, in October and November; A. E. Kreider, Life of Christ, November to

1. *Bulletin, MBS,* January, 1946, pp. 5-7.
2. *Bulletin,* November, 1945, p. 6.

February; and Harry Yoder, Church Organization and Administration, March to May. A similar list was proposed for the following year. Warkentin himself was teaching History and Message of the Old Testament throughout the year in the Bible School. Practical work for students was being arranged with Mennonite missions in the city and with surrounding churches.

One problem which loomed on the horizon, but which was not an immediate concern, was that of student housing. Classroom space was sufficient, and Bethany had plans for a chapel building which would further supplement that. Mennonite students, for the first year, were being housed in the Bethany apartments, but it was anticipated that the ending of the war and the imminent closing of C.P.S. camps would bring increased enrolment for both schools. The Bethany student rooms, already completely filled, could not be expected to accommodate Mennonite students. The search for a Mennonite home and the financial implications of this search then became a major matter for attention.

Progress in meeting the needs and work of the school year was interrupted unexpectedly before the month was over by a letter from the President to his Administrative Committee, which opened with the distressing words:

It is with real heavy heart that I sit down to write these lines to you. I know the Lord is leading and even though I do not yet understand His ways, I have full confidence in Him.

The letter continued with a report of abdominal pains, the doctor's diagnosis of a tumor and the need of immediate hospitalization and operation. This was the beginning of a series of attacks that eventually ended his service, though intervals of active participation in seminary developments were still to come.

The first hospitalization lasted from November 1 to December 6, and was followed by several more weeks of recuperation. In the meantime C. E. Krehbiel took over responsibilities for the work with the office assistance of Ruth Ewert. After Warkentin's return home, she made daily visits with reports on office matters and, after consultation, carried out much of the details of operation. By January Warkentin reported that the Lord had restored health to the point where he could spend a few hours each day in the office. Soon after he was busily engaged in seminary problems, especially that of housing. This activity was again interrupted with another hospitalization with surgery in February but by the time of the Board meeting in March, Warkentin was again active and giving full attention to work of the Seminary. It could be added here that further periods of hospitalization came the following year, one in June for twelve days and a final one in August which was a terminal illness.

The amazing thing in these last two years of Dr. Warkentin's service was his complete trust in the Lord with continual thanks and with immediate return to activity after each illness. His example gave a unique spiritual emphasis characteristic of the early years of the Seminary.

In these two years, the institution met three recurring problems for which at least the beginning of a solution was made. The first was that of housing, the second was that of affiliation or independent operation, and the third was that of staff.

Housing

The very existence of the school for another year hinged on finding space for living and operation. There were many possibilities for purchasing property, but securing occupation was more difficult due to wartime shortage of housing. Desirable apartment houses in the Bethany vicinity were available for purchase, but their usefulness would depend on legal action to evict tenants, which might or might not be successful and in any case would be unpleasant. That option was dropped after examining a few possibilities.

The next likely proposal was the purchase of one of the large old-time residences. A million dollar mansion, known as the Stout property, was first examined. Its earlier splendor and ample room were evident, but the Board's offer of $100,000 was too late. It had already been sold for $150,000. A similar South Side mansion, the Loeb property, seemed suitable, but the local residents objected and the Seminary deal was called off.

Headquarters Building, 4614 Woodlawn Avenue

It was after these events that the brown stone mansion at 4614 Woodlawn Avenue came to the attention of the Board in June 1946. The three-story home was backed by a carriage house, a caretaker's home, and far in the rear a large two-story garage, all surrounded by a beautifully landscaped lawn. On August 14, 1946, the home, along with the furniture and equipment, became the property of Mennonite Biblical Seminary for $47,000. Oil paintings later appraised for $50,000 decorated the home interior but were not left with the building.

One can hardly imagine the elation with which Dr. Warkentin and the Seminary family, so long without a square foot of tangible property, viewed the acquisition of this beautiful home. It was commodious and usable for student residence and, with some remodeling of the garage buildings, provided four apartments for married families. With the fall of 1946, 4614 Woodlawn Avenue became the headquarters address for the Seminary and the center of school activities. A dedication service was held on October 16, with Board members present as well as friends, faculty, and students. This, the speaker said, quoting Jacob, "is none other but the house of God and the gate to heaven."[1] It is a place for a vision of God, a place of refreshing for service, a place of rich fellowship.

It should be added that even before occupation of the new home, further space for office, library, conference room, and auditorium was found in the nearby Swedenborgian church where the church members, now moved farther away, were ready to rent the educational unit of their building. It was generally agreed that the first year's efforts in the matter of housing had been reasonably successful. Though the goal was not quite realized at the time, a basis had been laid for future development.

Affiliation

As to the question whether the institution was to be affiliated or independent, the answer had not been clearly found. This question had been somewhat related to the

1. Gen. 28:17; *Bulletin*, Oct. 1946, p. 6-7.

matter of housing, and especially when the commodious million dollar Stout property seemed available, movement in the direction of a completely independent school appeared as a real possibility. No later property examined warranted quite that vision; for some this was taken as the leading of God.

The Board, on July 31, 1945, had adopted the somewhat ambiguous recommendation of a Special Committee; this recommendation could be quoted on either side of the question. It read:

> That our Mennonite Seminary and Bible School be set up alongside and in affiliation with Bethany Biblical Seminary and Bethany Bible Training School in Chicago, which represents one of the historic peace churches . . . is fully accredited, has a Biblio-centered curriculum, and emphasizes the peace principle, rural life, and church music. . . . That our Seminary Board aim to set up our own institution with our own charter, name, faculty, catalog, curriculum, degrees and diplomas so that our students graduate from our own institution. However if . . . this is not immediately possible, our students shall enrol at Bethany Biblical Seminary until such time as this can be done.

It was in accord with the first part that the arrangements were made with Bethany in the fall of 1945. It was in accord with the second part that Dr. Warkentin felt he should be "looking forward to the establishment of our own institution as soon as possible." He himself became convinced that the affiliation as accomplished had been of the Lord's leading. It had given a satisfactory start in an accredited study; it had contributed cordial fellowship, in a spiritual atmosphere, with a church whose ministerial ideal was similar to that of the Mennonites.

The students in a memo to the Board meeting on March 13, 1946, expressed appreciation for the similarity in cultural ideals of the two schools, the Christian fellowship, and the sincere hospitality of Bethany. They approved the affiliation as fortunate. The general idea was that while an independent institution was the eventual aim, for the present this affiliation offered the best solution. What emerged then was neither complete submersion in a Bethany operation nor complete independence. There were two institutions in name with a common educational experience but separate administration. Mennonite students were enroled in Bethany after being registered and sponsored by Mennonite Biblical Seminary. Credits were recorded by Bethany and degrees were granted under the Bethany name. Extra curricular activities and matters of discipline or practical work and ministerial recommendations were Mennonite responsibility. With little modification the affiliation program as worked out in the first year served well for a decade, though in the face of occasional criticism.

Staff

The meager staff of one administrator-teacher, four part-time lecturers, and an office secretary was obviously not adequate for satisfactory operation. First attention was given to plans for more full-time representation in the Seminary faculty. Along with the other immediate concerns the March Board meeting had authorized a communication by cable to S. F. Pannabecker, then in China, to return for service as dean of the Seminary in the fall of 1946. Though no immediate reply was possible, he was able to join the staff in August. Another need, very pressing, developed as the housing problem was pursued: Someone must assist in the business office and with the many problems of property oversight and remodeling. John T. Neufeld, in charge of the Mennonite Bible Mission in Chicago, had earlier come to the city to study architecture; he turned out to be an admirable candidate for business manager and accepted a part-time position in June. His later service in business and rebuilding was invaluable.

With the pressure of mounting financial obligations a field representative was an urgent need. For this a call was issued to Edmund J. Miller, pastor of the Lind, Washington, Menno Church. He responded with some assistance in the summer and joined the staff in September 1946. Others, added during the following year, should be mentioned. Don E. Smucker, with experience in the pastorate and peace movements, responded to a call to the faculty and joined the staff in the summer of 1947 to teach in Biblical

Theology and Christian Ethics. Marvin J. Dirks, while studying music at Northwestern University, gave part-time instruction in voice during the first year and then became a faculty member in 1947 with responsibility for voice, choir, and the direction of practical work. As his last faculty addition, Dr. Warkentin invited and secured the services of Miss Katie Andres as librarian; she assumed her duties in the fall of 1947.

Readjustment and Expansion

Dr. Warkentin passed away on August 30, 1947. The loss of a devoted leader marked the end of a two-year period of beginnings. Though brief, it had been sufficient to set patterns of operation that were followed in the succeeding years. The seminary experience in Chicago was to last until 1958, a total of thirteen years, after which a new program was to be inaugurated. The Chicago years might be charterized in four periods as:

(1) 1945 — 1947 The Beginning — Setting patterns
(2) 1947 — 1951 Property expansion — rounding out a geographical base
(3) 1951 — 1954 Developed program — staff, students, and community
(4) 1954 — 1958 Approaching change

As already noted, the first two years under President Warkentin had seen the inauguration of an affiliated program with Bethany Biblical Seminary, the first steps in locating a seminary home, and the initial gathering of a staff. In regard to affiliation and location, there were to be recurring discussions and expressed disagreement, though in actual operation no other solution was found for a decade.

The funeral and memorial service for Dr. Warkentin occurred on September 2, at the opening of the new school year. Moving statements of high regard and esteem for his leadership were expressed. A letter from the Seminary Fellowship to the Board and friends characterized the attitude of all. It said in part:

We shall greatly miss his wise counsel and direction as well as the contagion of his deep and bouyant faith. It is, however, not our desire to stop with this lamentation over our loss, but rather to resolve to go forward with greater zeal and purpose than heretofore in living the life of humble Christian service to Christ and His Church, an ideal Dr. Warkentin so valiantly upheld for us all.[1]

In this same spirit the Seminary Board met the same day to consider means of carrying on the work. The staff was left temporarily in charge of administration, with Dean S. F. Pannabecker as chairman. At the same time a call was given to Rev. A. E. Kreider, Board member and former professor at Witmarsum, to serve as President. Though he considered the call seriously, Kreider's reply was negative, pleading health and the pressure of other responsibilities, especially that of chairman of the Board of Foreign Missions. With this move thwarted, the Board in their January 1948, meeting turned to the Dean with a call to the presidency. Thus S. F. Pannabecker became the second President of Mennonite Biblical Seminary and served until 1958. The staff otherwise remained the same.

Church Building and Offices, 4600 Woodlawn Avenue

1. *Seminary Bulletin,* September, 1947, p. 5-6.

Property Expansion

Purchase of the quarters at 4614 Woodlawn in 1946 did not completely solve the housing problem even that year. The seminary population numbered forty-seven in February 1947, including students, faculty members and their families. Thirty-two of these were housed in seminary property, eleven more in two Mennonite missions, and four in the Bethany dormitory. Increasing numbers were anticipated in the following years and actually the seminary community did number fifty-seven in 1948 and up to one hundred in 1949. It was this kind of expansion for which preparation was needed.

The Woodlawn Avenue area in which the Seminary had located was at the time facing a change. It had been an old high-class neighborhood but the older residents had passed away and their children had moved to other sections. The racial barrier, once protected by restrictions written into contracts limiting sale to white owners only, had fallen with the Supreme Court decision nullifying all such clauses. Newcomers, many nonwhite, were moving in and the color line was but a few blocks away. Woodlawn property, still beautiful and located but a short distance from the lake, with convenient transportation, could be purchased advantageously. One after another, the neighboring buildings and lots came into Seminary possession until all adjacent property in the 4600 block came to be a unit as a Seminary campus. This was accomplished in the years from 1947 to 1951.

Details of the various deals are not necessary. They followed much the same pattern, yet each had its own story. Demand for additional housing was pressing; nearby property was available. Each new purchase caused searching of heart as to whether the financial obligations were warranted; with some promises and more faith the needs were met and, without undue indebtedness, the transactions were carried through. Eventually all was paid for and, to complete the story, eventually all was sold again without loss.

The extent of property accumulated by the Seminary is shown graphically in the accompanying plate. The relationship of the buildings, their date of purchase, and the

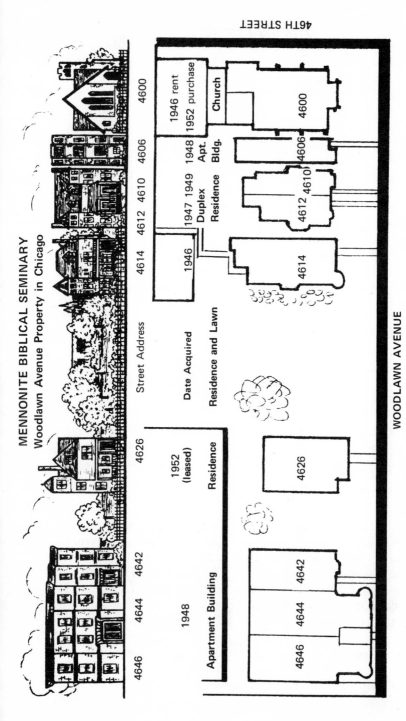

MENNONITE BIBLICAL SEMINARY
Woodlawn Avenue Property in Chicago

46TH STREET

	4646	4644	4642		4626		Street Address		4614	4612	4610	4606	4600
		1948			1952 (leased)		Date Acquired		1946	1947	1949	1948	1946 rent 1952 purchase
	Apartment Building				Residence		Residence and Lawn			Duplex	Residence	Apt. Bldg.	Church

WOODLAWN AVENUE

In this property there were 36 apartments for families and 27 rooms for single students, also laundry, storage, vault. Included also were facilities for offices, library, committee rooms, auditorium, sanctuary. Other buildings not shown provided apartments for non-seminary or university students and a mission center with apartments and public rooms.

amounts involved are indicated. The buildings were often designated by the name of the previous owner but can be indicated more conveniently by the address number on Woodlawn Avenue. The headquarters building, once the "Joyce Property," is simply 4614, so with others.

The purchase of each building was accompanied by a specific financial appeal, either to individuals or on a wider constituency basis. The purchase of 4612, for instance, occurred soon after locating on Woodlawn while other involvements were heavy. It was made possible by a loan from the Franz brothers in Lind, Washington — a loan which was later made an outright gift. That building was then often called "Franz Hall." For 4606 a special gift was received from the Henry G. Stauffer estate and the first floor of that building then designated as "Stauffer Apartments." The Central Conference made a special gift toward the church building as a memorial to Joseph Stucky, their founder. The main support came from church-wide solicitation. In the case of the church purchase the agreement to pay $27,500 in three months when there was practically nothing in hand seemed preposterous. A letter campaign was devised based on three points: (1) prayer participation by all — seminary family, Board members, and givers — seeking deeper devotion in all life (2) church-wide interest with gifts from all sections of the church, some larger but many small gifts (3) economy in raising funds with all contributions going to the church purchase. Students and staff, after a prayer service, assisted in a concerted effort of folding letters, stuffing envelopes, and mailing. The response was good and the obligations were met.

The church purchase in 1952 was the last major property acquisition. An average of one building a year had been added to the Seminary campus. The total capital investment up to January 1953, was $265,000 and of that only $35,000 indebtedness remained.[1] The business manager reported total contributions for capital and operating expenses for the years from September 1945, to the end of May 1953, had been $475,879.41.

Housing accommodations came to include thirty-six

---

1. *Bulletin,* January, 1954, p. 3, JTN "A Work of Faith."

apartments of varying size and twenty-seven single rooms. Two other buildings came into the Seminary circle, that at 1228 46th Street, one-half block east of the campus, which was purchased by special grant for the use of non-seminary students; and the Mission Center, at 4609 Woodlawn Avenue, just across from the Seminary buildings. Residents in these buildings also became part of the wider seminary family.

Staff

Although housing was a pressing problem, in the long run the staff, especially faculty members, was more important and more difficult to find. They could not be picked up at bargain prices. This was early realized and a goal of a minimum of four properly qualified professors was set with the hope that five could be secured. After the first few initial years, a Faculty Planning Committee was named by the Board and a more consistent search made for suitable persons. Over the years really able members of faculty and staff were accumulated but it was 1954 before claim to four effective faculty members could be made.

The full-time faculty members who served during the Woodlawn era numbered seven, with full-time (FT), part-time (pt), or absence on leave (lv) as noted:

Faculty	For the year beginning in the fall of												
	1945	46	47	48	49	50	51	52	53	54	55	56	57
A. Warkentin, President	FT	FT											
S. F. Pannabecker, Dean or President		FT	FT	FT	FT	FT	FT	FT	FT	FT	FT	FT	FT
D. E. Smucker, Christian Ethics			FT	FT	lv	FT	FT	FT	FT	FT	FT	FT	
M. J. Dirks, Voice and Choir			pt	pt	pt	FT	FT	FT	FT	FT	FT	FT	FT
J. J. Enz, Old Testament								pt	lv	FT	FT	FT	FT
Katie Andres, Librarian	FT	FT	FT	FT	FT	FT	FT						
Magdalen Friesen, Librarian										FT	FT	FT	FT
Erland Waltner													FT

The president taught about a one-half teaching load but was numbered with the teaching faculty. The librarians were recognized as faculty members but not counted toward teaching faculty. Don E. Smucker began in 1947 as a teacher in the Bible School but soon began teaching in the graduate seminary and proved a very popular lecturer. Marvin Dirks started as part-time teacher of voice and

MBS Staff, 1947-51
back row: Katie Andres, John T. Neufeld, Sylvia Pannabecker
front row: Don E. Smucker, S. F. Pannabecker, Marvin Dirks

before long began teaching in the field of choral music. His seminary choirs toured the country and made favorable impressions in music and testimony. Jacob J. Enz finally provided the fourth professor and proved to be a stimulating voice in the Old Testament field. In the last year at Woodlawn, Erland Waltner joined the faculty as teacher in New Testament but more important as President-elect for the following year. There were others who gave part-time to teaching or assisting for shorter periods, such as Leland and Bertha Harder and Erna Fast, as well as many who came in for special teaching for one quarter.

Other members of the staff serving in administration were important:

Administrative Staff	For the year beginning in the fall of
	1945 46 47 48 49 50 51 52 53 54 55 56 57
John T. Neufeld, Business Manager	pt pt pt pt pt pt pt pt pt
E. J. Miller, Field Secretary	FT pt
Andrew R. Shelly, Dir. of Public Relations	pt pt pt pt FT FT FT lv FT FT FT
C. J. Dyck, Business Manager	pt pt

The significance of John T. Neufeld has been mentioned. Although serving part-time, he handled a full-time position effectively. His knowledge of the city and enthusiasm for Chicago inspired many students to a long-time interest in urban church work. A heart attack at the opening of the 1955-56 school year kept him out of his office temporarily. He returned later for work but in the following year requested relief from his post. His resignation was accepted with deep appreciation for his work in ten critical years.

Two men gave outstanding service in field work. E. J. Miller visited churches and aroused support during a two-year period when he also completed his seminary course. He had been pastor at Lind, Washington, and was the key to securing the special help which came at critical times from that wheat farming area. Andrew R. Shelly was the long-time field man and Director of Public Relations. His first service was a contribution of his congregation at Kitchener, Ontario, who gave him three months leave on full salary to travel for the Seminary. After finding a suitable successor for his pastorate, Shelly was able to join the staff on a full-time basis, working in public relations and teaching in the field of church administration and Mennonite polity. As an interpreter of the Seminary to the church and the church to the Seminary, he performed a task of inestimable value.

Other staff members, especially the secretaries, performed tasks far more important than their lack of publicity suggests. Frieda Claassen — first on a temporary basis, then as regular office secretary — has by now given longer full-time service than any other Seminary employee. She began work in 1947 and served through all of the Woodlawn years as well as after the later move. She perhaps knows more students and graduates than any administrator or faculty member. Esther Neufeld Kressly long assisted her father as cashier and when he was ill, practically took over his work. Not least important, though one of the last, was C. J. Dyck who, while taking graduate work, accepted the position of Business Manager and carried that office the last two years at Woodlawn and during the transfer to Elkhart. Others also, for longer or shorter periods, filled the important posts of matron, hostess, dietician, or janitor. The overall janitorial supervision was under Walter Verderber who, with his mother, wife, and son, lived in the basement apartment at 4642. He was a large, powerful figure, always accommodating, whom many will remember watching the various heating plants or cleaning off winter's snow with his powered plow.

Students

The Seminary existed for the training of ministerial students and the student population was watched with greatest interest. Both graduate seminary and Bible school students were counted in the total number. Those in the Bible School, however, decreased from a high of six the first year to only two or three after 1948; there were none in 1952-53 and only occasional part-time thereafter. There were also part-time auditors each year, often wives of students or faculty, who visited one or two classes but usually not for credit. Their number is given in parentheses in the table below, and is also included in the total figures. The enrolment varied slightly for each quarter of the year, but the overall figures for each year are given below. The

STUDENT ENROLMENT. Mennonite Biblical Seminary

	Total No.	Men	Women	BD	MRE	MTh	ED	CD	WD	ND	PD	Can	Frn	Oth	Non-Sem. Stud.	(1)	(2)	(3)
1945-46	18	13	5		2		1	2	10		3		1	1				
1946-47	26	20	6	2	1		1	4	9	3	7		1		1			
1947-48	23	16	7	1			7	8	2	4			2	1	6	41	16	57
1948-49	33	25	8	9			1	10	8	6	2	3	2	1	8	74	27	101
1949-50	(5) 29	18(5)	11	4	3	1		4	9	10			4	1	1	14	83	25	108
1950-51	(5) 47	30(9)	17	4	2	1	1	3	14	8	5	6	4	1	8	84	22	106
1951-52	44	33	11	8	3		4	4	10	11	4	8	1	2	13	93	24	117
1952-53	35	29	6	9			6	5	10	4	3	5	3		16	99	27	126
1953-54	(3) 48	36(3)	12	11	2		1	8	14	10	1	9	4	1	12	114	30	144
1954-55	36	32	4	7	4	1	1	6	6	6	3	8	2	3	14	103	29	132
1955-56	(9) 44	31(9)	13	9	1		2	11	9	8	3	8	3		13	101	33	134
1956-57	(3) 34	26(3)	8	3	2		2	7	8	8		7	1	1	17	95	23	118
1957-58	(9) 49	30(9)	19	10	1		1	11	12	11		13		1	12	97	26	123

NOTE:

Figures in parenthesis are the number of part-time students included in the figure following.

Of graduates there were also 2 Bachelor of Sacred Literature from the Bible School, 1 each in 1947 and 1950.

Under Source are the different districts also Can=Canada, Frn=Foreign, Oth=Other Mennonite Groups or other denominations.

Under Residents: (1) is number of Adults (2) number of Children (3) Total.

Data for students is taken from the annual Catalog lists. The data for Non-seminary students and Residents is from the annual September list of residents.

smallest number was eighteen for the first year and the largest was forty-eight in 1953-54. Representatives came from every district of the United States and Canada with one or more foreign students every year. Most students came from the General Conference, but a few other Mennonites attended as did an occasional member of other Protestant denominations. The table summarizes the figures.

A total of 198 students registered for full-time work at Mennonite Biblical Seminary in Chicago over the thirteen years. In addition twenty-eight, mostly wives, took part-time work of a few hours. The women enroled for full-time work usually constituted about one-fourth of the full-time enrolment. The Western District, being the largest in membership, was usually represented by more students than any other with the Northern or Central District placing second. Considering the distance, however, the Pacific District was at times represented by a surprising number. Canadian students began to come in the early years, first in fewer numbers, but becoming almost one-third of the student body at the end.

Each year had one or more foreign students. Ernst Harder from Paraguay was present the first year; Leo

MBS Graduating Class of 1950
left to right: Henry Grimm, Ronald von Riesen, Marie Kroeker, Erwin Goering
Sarah Mae Wiens, Harold Ratzlaff, Erna Friesen, Marvin Dirks, Orlin Frey

Laurense from Holland, the second year; and a few years later Andre Goll from France. All have since become prominent figures in their homelands. Some others stayed in the U.S. or returned to become long-time residents of this land, e.g., Grace Liu Yang from China, Franco Cosco from Italy, Margaret Fehderau Ediger from Brazil, Gerrit Veendorp of Holland, and Herman and Jo Tan from Indonesia. All of them helped introduce American students to other cultures and ideals.

Non-seminary Residents

Parallel with the seminary student body was a group of university or medical students who found residence in Seminary apartments. One of the buildings had been subsidized by the Home Mission Board especially for them. In addition, as other room was available, more were accepted. They averaged perhaps a dozen each year and, with wives and children, made a sizeable proportion of the seminary family. Among these were some who were most active in Seminary community affairs and church life and later in conference work. One need only mention such names as Roland Brown, Eldon Graber, Robert Kreider, Howard Shelly, Alden Voth, Otto Klassen, and Elmer Neufeld to realize the contribution they would make to the Seminary fellowship.

To the Seminary families and the university student families were added another group of residents. Some who happened to be living in the buildings when they were bought remained. Others were accepted to fill unoccupied room. All were congenial. Frank King and his wife, long time Mennonite residents of Chicago, occupied an apartment for his last years in the city before retiring. They aided much in community relations and understanding city life. The total population of the wider Seminary family numbered up to one hundred forty and about thirty being children of the different family groups. The Seminary world was a little microcosm in the big city.

The Seminary Program

It was in the academic life that affiliation with Bethany Biblical Seminary found expression. The Bethany curricu-

Combined MBS-Bethany Faculty, 1956
back row: Wieand, Mow, Beahm, Dirks, Brightbill, Ziegler, Faw, Mallott
front row: Smucker, Pannabecker, Robinson, Enz, Franz

MBS Student Body, September 1953

lum of 1945 became the Mennonite curriculum with the addition of a few special courses by visiting lecturers. Pannabecker, Smucker, and Dirks joined the Bethany staff so that they worked as a single faculty. Similarly, on the student level, those from the Mennonite group were inducted into the Bethany classes and all students formed a single student body for instructional purposes. Mennonite faculty were assigned courses in their specialties — Pannabecker in Christianity in America and the Far East; Smucker, Christian Ethics; and Dirks, Voice and Choral Music. The curriculum was essentially the Bethany curriculum with the usual four departments of Bible, Theology, Church History, and the Practical Field. As a Biblical seminary, Bethany had long emphasized the Biblical field but in the recent years new emphasis had been placed on Church Work and the courses in Mental Hygiene and Counseling were proving popular.

A hearty welcome was extended by both Bethany faculty and students to their new Mennonite colleagues. The similarity of background, both religious and cultural, promoted easy relationships. The weekly faculty prayer meetings and the daily chapel services, with the common noonday meal, gave rise to a close and inspiring fellowship. The Mennonites were invited to, and many joined in, the annual Brethren love feast and communion service. There probably was no other seminary in the country where as pleasant a relationship could have been set up.

The question was early raised as to just what Mennonite emphasis should be expected in such an affiliated program. Discussion generally settled on two points: that a larger impact in instruction was desirable, and that certain areas, which met criticism from the constituency, should be reviewed. The latter pertained to the nature of instruction in the Biblical field, especially Old Testament. The immediate answer to both of these seemed to be an increase in the Mennonite faculty. The long-time answer seemed to be a shift from the affiliated relationship to one which might be characterized as "federated" in which two fully equipped schools, each accredited, joined forces in a common program. Since the latter was out of the question at the moment, it was left for a later day and efforts were concentrated on enlarging the faculty.

It was under these circumstances that the Faculty Planning Committee was organized and soon J. J. Enz was invited to serve in the field of Old Testament. His actual participation was delayed a year by a bout with polio but he joined the staff in 1954. At the same time Erland Waltner was invited but his acceptance was postponed for several years. A few others were also invited but none responded for full service. A gift of sufficient copies of the *Mennonite Hymnary* for the Bethany chapel may have been an attempt to bolster the Mennonite presence; more significant was an addition of a sequence of Mennonite studies to the curriculum in 1953. A prerequisite was college study of general Mennonite History. This was to be followed by three basic courses: I. Anabaptist-Mennonite Faith and Theology; II. American Mennonites and the General Conference Mennonite Church; III. Mennonite Missions and World Service. These with other Anabaptist studies were primarily for Mennonite students but occasionally were taken by others also.

Bus Transportation to Bethany

Seminary Life

The Mennonite fellowship was nourished by extracurricular activities. Even the problem of traveling eleven miles by Seminary bus from Woodlawn to the Bethany campus, although burdensome at times, provided a period of fellowship and at one time this trip was used by J. J. Enz as occasion for an elementary Hebrew class. Vesper services were started in February of 1947 and held monthly at first and occasionally thereafter. These were an occasion for the gathering of all city Mennonites. More specifically for students was the annual, or semiannual, retreat. At times only students gathered for meditation and directed discussion; at other times it became a family affair. The beautiful little chapel at the Community Center Foundation as Palos Park, near Chicago, was the scene of some of these retreats; others were held as far away as Camp Friedenswald in Michigan. A Seminary Council with representatives from all of the groups living at Woodlawn was organized; it concerned itself with student problems and student obligations to the community.

The Seminary location provided a convenient center for many conference and committee meetings and introduced students to the whole range of General Conference and Mennonite Church (MC) activities. The Council of Boards met twice at the Seminary, first in 1948 and again in 1950. The Central Conference ministers often held an annual retreat at the Seminary. The officers of the Young People's Union likewise met in the Woodlawn church parlor.

Four significant study conferences were held at the Woodlawn quarters. A conference on City Missions and Churches was held in April 1951, sponsored jointly by the Seminary and the General Conference Board of Missions. All in the Seminary were invited to join in the study of the "predicament and opportunity" of city work. An All-District Peace Committee Conference in October 1951, brought in leaders from the Mennonite (MC), Brethren, and General Conference groups. A study conference on The Mennonite Minister and His Training was authorized by the Seminary Board and held in October 1953. It was preceded by careful preparation, and focused on the presentation of four papers pertaining to the New Testament basis, the

Faculty Retreat at Palos Park

minister's task, current trends in theological education, and the place of the Mennonite minister. Discussion then centered on academic and spiritual preparation.[1] Perhaps the most significant of all was the 1955 Conference on the Believers' Church which marked a crucial point in the whole church's thinking on the nature of the church. The meetings with the delegation of five Russian Baptists who were repaying an earlier Mennonite visit to Russia were held in the Seminary church building for two days in May 1956.

Woodlawn Mennonite Church

Of all the non-curricular activities no doubt that which was most significant was the organization of the Woodlawn Mennonite Church. Such a step had been foreseen as early as 1945 in Seminary Board discussion but its practical stimulus came in an unexpected way. Hanno Klassen, a foreign student at the seminary, of Mennonite background

1. *The Bulletin,* January, 1954, p. 4ff.

but never baptized, requested baptism in April 1949. While a little Sunday school had been in operation, no steps had been taken toward organizing a church fellowship. The question then was who should baptize Hanno and under what auspices and into what congregation. Perhaps all of the concentration on details was unnecessary, but it did lead to his baptism at the hands of Don Smucker, the organization of a Seminary Fellowship in October 1949, and a temporary church organization in the following year. The resulting Woodlawn Mennonite Church was definitely a Seminary church. Faculty and students labored over the constitution, bylaws and organization. On January 28, 1951, sixteen regular members were accepted and forty-two associate members. All were residents of the Seminary community but others were invited and the church came to include neighborhood people. Its activities gave Seminary students an unusual opportunity to work in a definite city community and to struggle with the problems of a small but growing church. Students served as pastors until Rev. J. N. Smucker responded to a call and accepted the position on a part-time basis in September 1952, with student assistance.

Over the years from 1950 to 1958 eight students were involved as part-time pastor or assistant pastor of the Woodlawn Church. Others served in various church offices, and the whole group was engaged in a growing community program. Country-bred students learned the joys and tragedies of urban work. They entertained city-bred children in weekly play hours on the Seminary lawn; they were frustrated by boys hiding under the church benches in released-time religious instruction; they sponsored one boy who got in trouble with the law for stealing a bicycle. Later he repented and after probation, requested to join the church and was one of the first black boys to be accepted. All this was in addition to neighborhood visitation and the usual Sunday school and worship program.

Over a dozen of the neighborhood residents were gradually drawn into active association and about half of them became members of the church. When the time came for the Seminary to leave Woodlawn, the church had fifty-one regular members, of whom thirty-four were local people, eleven having been accepted at Easter, 1958. Delton Franz

Organization Meeting of Woodlawn Mennonite Church, January 28, 1951

Accepting new Members, Woodlawn Mennonite Church, 1957

54

was the pastor and a black student from the University; Vincent Harding was assistant pastor. The work appeared encouraging enough to be retained under support of the General Conference Board of Missions with the prospect of developing an integrated congregation. Unfortunately later developments militated against the hoped-for results.

Approaching Change

The years around 1955 represent the matured Woodlawn experience. The campus had been established, student body gathered, and the affiliated program geared to a more creditable Mennonite participation. There was a sense of accomplishment, a growing body of alumni and supporters, and a hopeful prospect. There were, however, certain signs, not necessarily disturbing but at least thought-provoking, that this program could not be the permanent form of General Conference Mennonite ministerial training. The "affiliated" relationship had been criticized from the beginning and needed rethinking. Occasional discussions with Bethany Biblical Seminary had broached the subject and there was openness to reconsidering the program. The matter of accreditation had been raised and had received some encouragement.

Incidental factors encouraged and even necessitated more serious attention to future plans. The most obvious was the changing Woodlawn community. By this time the white residents, except for a few hard-core holdouts, had left and were being replaced by new black residents. The move was accelerated by mammoth new housing construction to the north which was driving tenants to relocate. The replacement of white by black was not bad in itself, but the doubling and trebling of population overcrowded the schools and forced children onto the streets. The adjacent Shakespeare School, once with 800 white pupils and a few black, grew to 2400 black pupils with an occasional white. The uneasiness experienced in night time travel increased. A few disturbances occurred in Seminary buildings. Faculty members with young children either sent them to private schools or themselves moved out to the suburbs. As a consequence, the Seminary had to operate from three bases instead of two. Smucker and Dirks had moved to York

Center, classwork was at Bethany, and the Seminary home was at Woodlawn. The whole group seldom got together.

Changes in administration were also in the making. S. F. Pannabecker, President since 1948, indicated his desire to retire from administration at the age of sixty which was but a year away. Rufus D. Bowman, long-time President of Bethany, had passed away in 1952 and had been replaced by Paul Robinson. The Bethany group had sealed their decision to remain in their old location by building a new chapel in 1951, but the new President and the social changes similar to those at Woodlawn were raising the question again. Both schools were in a situation of flux.

For Mennonite Biblical Seminary — Board, faculty, students, and friends — there were anxious moments and repeated discussions. Three options seemed to be present: (1) to go ahead with an affiliated program somewhat as before, but this was largely ruled out from the beginning (2) to reconsider a new effort at an independent program at some suitable location (3) to work out a new associated program on an equal basis rather than on affiliation. The last seemed most desirable and was being considered as a possibility with Bethany in some new location suitable for development.

It was in this situation that a new possibility arose in a rather unexpected fashion. Relations with the Mennonite (MC) seminary at Goshen College had been cultivated in various ways and had led to friendly exchanges. In 1953 a joint summer school was proposed and actually came to pass in the summer of 1954. It was held at Goshen College and attracted students from various Mennonite groups with faculty members representing both Goshen and Woodlawn.

The joint summer school was repeated in 1955, this time located at Woodlawn. By this time Mennonite Biblical Seminary was being presented a new alternative. Attractive as the Bethany relationship had been, there was growing appeal for an inter-Mennonite effort. Eventually this was the course taken for the two schools, though the way was complicated and at times uncertain. This is another story which belongs in the next chapter.

The Woodlawn era of Mennonite Biblical Seminary ended in the summer of 1958, but up until that time the program was carried on with no relaxation and with a sense of accomplishment. The graduation of the last class and the closing exercises of the last Mennonite-Bethany year were serious occasions for both schools. Expressions of appreciation and regret at parting were heard. Both were soon to relocate — Bethany at Oakbrook, Mennonite at Elkhart — with different paths but a hopeful future and occasional convergence of ways.

4

EMERGENCE OF A NEW PROGRAM

Joint Summer Session, 1954

The two Mennonite seminaries, one at Goshen and one at Chicago, had had a nodding acquaintance with each other prior to 1954. There had been an occasional exchange of speakers and a joint Anabaptist Seminar with some recognition of common interests but no attempt to relate the two programs. The joint summer session held in 1954 was an innovation in that it was a formal cooperative venture. It did not at the time imply any closer organizational connection, though it provided the opportunity for such thoughts to be expressed.

The six-weeks summer session centered on the Goshen campus under the leadership of H. S. Bender with Mennonite (MC) teachers such as Howard Charles, J. C. Wenger, Gideon Yoder, and C. K. Lehman. From the General Conference side, Don E. Smucker and Erland Waltner taught courses and Robert Kreider and S. F. Pannabecker gave special lectures. The student enrolment was not large but included twenty from the Mennonites (MC) and five from the General Conference. Among the latter were Peter Dyck, David Schroeder, and James Reusser, all with previous inter-Mennonite interests and experience. They met a hearty welcome from the Goshen students. Two more, who were neither Mennonite (MC) nor General Conference, were particularly important — William Klassen and Calvin Redekop. They were Goshen seminary students and, not being tied to either side, they presented the most urgent plea for joint action. The Canadians in the two seminaries may well have been the prime stimulus in bringing about the summer session and the consideration of cooperation.

Through personal conversation and group discussion the sentiment crystallized that the time was at hand for something more tangible in cooperation in ministerial training. Dean H. S. Bender, probably recognizing this as the wave of the future, encouraged the discussion though nothing specific emerged at the moment. It was agreed to repeat the joint summer session in 1955 at Woodlawn campus.

This was the beginning of a series of events that culminated two years later in both seminary boards and both constituencies approving a cooperative venture that became the Associated Mennonite Biblical Seminaries. It would be of no credit to the negotiators nor honor to the Lord to imply that everything went smoothly and that there were no difficulties in reaching common understandings. There were misunderstandings; there were differences of opinion, and there were fears which, whether well based or not, were real and had to be met. Through it all, the persons involved were trying their best to understand each other and to meet sympathetically the desires and conditions laid down by other participants. It is with thanks to God that through the work of His Spirit, it was possible to reach eventually a common understanding and an acceptable program of cooperation. Subsequent results had justified the hopes in the venture that was attempted.

Looking back over the two years of search for a mutually agreeable program, there appear four rather definitely marked stages of discussion.

The first, sparked by the 1954 summer session, was one of **Exploration and Hope** with initial progress and a proposed plan.

The second, marked by initial publicity in the spring of 1955 and continuing throughout the year, was one of **Negotiation and Fear.** Questions were raised and negative reactions expressed; some of these seemed insurmountable.

The third, initiated by a new proposal in May of 1956, was one of **Accommodation and Understanding.** Though not entirely as originally hoped, the plan still offered reasonable assurance of success and seemed acceptable.

The fourth stage was marked by **Official Approval and**

Action. The General Conference session in August 1956, by formal resolution, approved the move, and shortly after this the Mennonite Board of Education gave similar official approval. After the way was thus cleared, active steps of preparation were taken toward inauguration of the program which was opened in September 1958. The story would not be complete without some reference to the developments at each stage.

Exploration and Hope

The 1954 summer discussions did not give rise to any continuation committee. If there were to be further follow-up, it was necessary for some individual to take up the cause. Erland Waltner stepped in at this time and with the sanction of the Seminary and Board administrative officers took responsibility personally for calling a meeting of interested persons. Waltner was himself a member of the Seminary Board and had been invited to serve on the Chicago faculty. While postponing decision on the matter, he was deeply interested in the Seminary's future. The meeting was held at the Atlantic Hotel in Chicago on October 9, 1954, and lasted from 9:30 a.m. to 4:45 p.m. Attendance was rather limited; there were nine present. Five were from the General Conference side — Waltner and Rosenberger from the Seminary Board and Pannabecker and Don Smucker from the Seminary, with William Snyder of Mennonite Central Committee. Four were from the Mennonite (MC) side — Nelson Kauffman, President of the Board of Education; Mininger and Bender from Goshen College and Seminary, with Orie O. Miller of the Mennonite Central Committee. None attended in any official capacity, yet they represented significant elements in their respective constituencies. Waltner was asked to chair the meeting and Bender to serve as secretary.

The purpose of the meeting was announced as an "exploratory discussion on the desirability and the feasibility of cooperation between Mennonite Biblical Seminary and Goshen Biblical Seminary." A broad suggestive agenda covered questions of possible advantages and problems, form of cooperation and location, next steps and timing. There was a generally favorable attitude. It was recognized that the two institutions should continue as independent organizations, not integrated too intimately at the beginning but cooperating especially in library and certain buildings. Three locations were suggested — Goshen, Elkhart, and Chicago — but it was emphasized that the Goshen Seminary would not be free to move at this time and the MBS Board would have to decide whether they would be willing to move to Goshen for an associated program. No difficulty was raised at the time as to location, though the General Conference men were not favorable to any college situation. Further steps were to be taken by the respective Boards after being informed of this preliminary discussion, and it was hoped other Mennonite groups might be interested.

Reports of the meeting, labeled "Confidential," were made to the concerned boards. The MBS Board, meeting two weeks after the exploratory group, was the first to reply and expressed favor and interest in continuing the

Sub-Committee of Four to Prepare Details of a Cooperative Program
left to right: Erland Waltner, S. F. Pannabecker, H. S. Bender, Paul Mininger

study. The members of the previous informal gathering were asked to continue. As a result, a second exploratory meeting with a few additional members was held on December 21, 1954; two meetings of a Sub-Committee of Four took place on the following January 1 and February 19, and a third meeting of the original Exploratory Committee on February 28, 1955. At this last meeting other Mennonite groups were invited to send representatives and their interest was shown by the presence of Reuben Short of the Evangelical Mennonite Church, H. H. Janzen of the Mennonite Brethren, A. P. Toews of the Evangelical Mennonite Brethren, and C. N. Hostetter, Jr., of the Brethren in Christ.

To the February 29 meeting was presented a Proposed Plan, largely the work of the Sub-Committee of Four. This smaller committee consisted of Erland Waltner, Chairman, H. S. Bender, Secretary; Paul Mininger; and S. F. Pannabecker. They had spent many hours in consultation, had corresponded, and had together inspected several plots on or near the Goshen College campus which might be regarded as suitable sites for the projected joint operation. In the interim, informal reports of the exploratory study had been made to various individuals and groups. The impressions gathered from these contacts were regarded as significant. They varied somewhat with the previous experience which the persons consulted had had with Mennonites not of their own group. There was perhaps a little more general favor toward a cooperative experiment on the part of the General Conference, though from the Mennonite side came many expressions of approval although with more tendency to proceed with caution. Neither Board had expressed themselves up to the time of this meeting except to approve study of the question. The February 28 meeting therefore was significant because of the presentation of a definite plan for consideration. Its reception would have much to do with the future direction.

The Proposed Plan can be reviewed briefly. It was read in detail at the Joint Exploratory Meeting and revised on several minor points, but it remained substantially as presented. **The Name** of the joint institution was to be the Associated Mennonite Biblical Seminaries. As a **Doctrinal Basis**, the Scriptures and the historic Anabaptist-Mennonite interpretation of them were accepted. **Organizational Relationships** provided for two independent degree-granting institutions, each offering its own full three-year course with separate administration but cooperating by mutual agreement. A Joint Coordinating Committee was to be responsible for supervision on the board level and a Joint Administrative Committee on the institutional level. A Joint Library Committee would administer the library. As to the **Integration of Work,** teachers and students were to be responsible to their own school and follow its prescribed curriculum. Common standards would be maintained and cross registration allowed in courses of the other school with the permission of the dean. Joint courses were envisioned in certain areas most suitable, such as languages, history, missions, and anthropology. Joint chapel services might be expected once a week and differing worship traditions would be respected. The **Location** was specified as in or near the city of Goshen but "outside the normal perimeter of the Goshen College campus." **Academic Buildings** would be provided for each institution, though joint use of certain facilities could be expected, and the buildings should be near enough to each other for academic integration.

This Plan of Cooperation was approved by the Exploratory Committee for presentation to the Boards of the two institutions, both of which were due to meet shortly. The Exploratory Committee and the Sub-Committee of Four had had a remarkable fellowship in preparation of the Plan. Differences of viewpoint had not marred a deeper commitment to Mennonite unity and cooperation. There was a sense of accomplishment and expectancy — a feeling that the Spirit was moving.

Response from the two boards came promptly. The Executive Committee of the Mennonite Board of Education met on March 1, and received a report of the discussions. They noted "the overtures of Mennonite Biblical Seminary for closer cooperation in seminary work" and the "probable readiness of MBS to locate in Goshen." The Executive Committee expressed welcome to MBS to join in this cooperative move. Final action, of course, was reserved for the Board itself. The Mennonite Biblical Seminary Board met on March 2 for their annual meeting and also reviewed the Plan. Their action expressed support of a move "along the general lines set out in the committee report." Some concern was added as to the Goshen location. A program of information and discernment of attitude of constituent bodies was authorized. Eventual referral to the General Conference was anticipated. In the meantime, the current affiliated program with Bethany Biblical Seminary was to be continued wholeheartedly.

At this point the first stage in the development of the Associated Mennonite Seminaries idea was completed. The Exploratory Committee regarded their work as concluded. The two Boards had reviewed the Plan and given a modest encouragement though with obvious reservations. Progress was about as could be expected, certainly positive and hopeful. Next moves awaited further reactions to the proposed plan. Clearance came from the Mennonite (MC) side by the middle of March when Mininger reported three district meetings with Board members. A straw vote had shown only one negative vote, three uncertain, and the rest, probably some thirty, all favorable.

Negotiations and Fear

The MBS Board inaugurated a rather detailed plan of reporting. A four-page progress report was prepared for circulation at each presentation with a three-fold stated purpose: (1) give information (2) provide opportunity for discussion and answer questions, and (3) ascertain reactions. It summarized the study as made up-to-date and outlined the plan. Regarding location which seemed the most tender point in the negotiations, it was stated:

> Our representatives have favored a location related to Chicago or else some center associated with a Mennonite community but not location on a college campus. The (Old) Mennonites have presented various reasons why they consider it not feasible to move to any other location than one in the vicinity of their present center, namely Goshen.

It was pointed out that the new program would solve the Woodlawn location problem, but added that that problem was not yet serious, that work could continue unabated and adequate time taken for discussion and decision. The decision must finally be made on the basis of the desirability of inter-Mennonite cooperation. The progress report expressed confidence in the Lord's leading up to this point and the assurance that with His further leading the future would hold something even better.

The first responses came from the General Conference Central Office staff, then the college faculties, and the Seminary family — faculty, students, and alumni. Questionnaires had been handed out and on return could be tabulated. As to the cooperative plan in principle, two-thirds were clearly favorable, the other third was divided half and half between those not favorable and those uncertain. As to the location question, which always arose, probably two-thirds regarded Goshen as a possible solution, even though unsatisfactory. Over one-fourth were unalterably opposed to the Goshen College campus location. Other objections to the plan were raised, e.g., the indefinite and rather limited amount of joint class work, the too strict division into two separate institutions, and the related impression that the MBS as a small group in the large college-seminary complex would be too submerged.

By July responses had been received in a general way, but not as definite, from the various district conferences. Here there was a pronounced negative reaction in only one area, viz., the Central District, closest to the proposed location. Even here, as in the other districts, there was still much support for the move. Objections, when expressed, were similar to those previously registered — location and loss of identity in particular. As one person expressed it, the arrangement would be like "living with the in-laws."

The Seminary President's progress report in July 1955, summarized his impression in three points:

(1) There is a great ground swell of popular interest in the idea of inter-Mennonite cooperation in seminary education and a sense that this is the proper direction to move.

(2) There is a large number, probably a big majority of informed persons — ministers, graduates, and church officers — favorable to this proposed plan, even though recognizing the validity of certain objections.

(3) There is a smaller number, definitely a minority, of

informed and intelligent persons who are opposed to the move on various grounds.

With this report of reactions the whole matter of further negotiations was turned back to the former Exploratory Committee and its Sub-Committee of Four. The Sub-Committee met four times between June and October 1955. In June and July they surveyed possible sites at Goshen and cleared up some misapprehensions, but found no other solution to location. A September meeting continued search for an acceptable alternative. During the discussions the possibility of Elkhart as a neutral location had been suggested but not actively promoted; it offered little promise of acceptance. Among the General Conference members of the Committee, sentiment was beginning to crystallize that the location question and the implications it had for "domination," "neutrality," and "mutuality" were much more significant than previously thought. H. S. Bender, as secretary of the September meeting, caught this feeling in his closing paragraph to the minutes:

> The meeting adjourned with the feeling of a better mutual understanding of the problems and difficulties, aware that it is possible, though not probable, that the plan may be rejected by either or both Boards.

A Western District Conference resolution which came in October was significant. It was positive in encouraging further study but added:

> Looking forward to the time when cooperation may be entered into freely and equally on neutral ground and not in any city where a Mennonite College is located. . . .

Toward the end of October came rather definitive actions. The Exploratory Committee presented a final report. They expressed appreciation for growth in understanding and fellowship, faith in the possibility of some kind of cooperative work, and consciousness of grave difficulties. In a ten-point summary they recognized the popular support for the program "in principle" and the real opposition on the basis of (1) location (2) organizational relationships, and (3) fear of domination. They reviewed the arguments pro and con and urged definite action along one of three lines — acceptance, rejection, or conditional approval with further study of possible modifications. The Mennonite Board of Education took action about this time approving the plan and welcoming Mennonite Biblical Seminary to the Goshen campus. It was left then for the MBS Board to act, which they did at the semi-annual meeting, October 25-26, 1955. Here the Board acknowledged receipt of a letter from President Paul Robinson of Bethany Biblical Seminary expressing readiness to enter a joint study of possible closer relationships of the two institutions. Reply was appreciative of the invitation but remarked that "the course of our future relationship in seminary education is not sufficiently clear to give a definite answer at this time." Main attention at the Board meeting was given to the Exploratory Committee report, and discussion was summed up in a resolution recognizing widespread interest in the inter-Mennonite cooperation plan and the sense that it was of God and should be realized. The resolution noted, however, such opposition to the location that, "the Board has not discerned the leading of God to be toward Goshen as a suitable location . . . and after much consideration and prayer would request and welcome further study in an attempt to find a location that would be mutually acceptable."

The most important meeting following this was a large gathering December 21-22 attended by nineteen from the General Conference Mennonite Church, fifteen from the Mennonite Church (MC), and five others from other branches. The stated purpose was not to present arguments pro and con, but rather frank explanation and searching for mutual understanding. Speakers for MBS pointed out that 20% of the constituency were adamantly opposed to the Goshen location and 50-75% opposed but willing to accept it only to save the cooperative program. Their fear was of excessive domination and pressure on a small minority by the overwhelming college-seminary community. The Goshen representatives explained that their seminary was still in process of winning its way among the constituency and that only recently would consideration of an inter-Mennonite plan have been possible; to now add to that the move away from Goshen would be too serious a strain on the developing support. Further, the college and seminary were felt to have mutual advantages in their association, and it would be a loss to both to move.

Long discussion and remarks by representatives of other groups still left a prime question much as previously stated. It was in this meeting that the proposal of an alternative location at Elkhart was presented by A. S. Rosenberger of the MBS Board. His group was open to this, and he hoped the Goshen group might find the ten-mile separation from Goshen not impossible. On adjournment of the day and a half discussions, the Secretary, H. S. Bender, added to the minutes:

> The general mood of the meeting as it closed was one of deep appreciation for the discussions, an awareness of the far-reaching significance of the meeting, and a warmer hope for ultimate success in the proposed inter-Mennonite seminary association.

In the months from January to April 1956, there were meetings and much correspondence in an attempt to find a solution. An Elkhart site was found which seemed suitable and favorable to Goshen transportation but failed to interest the Goshen group. There was more communication from concerned persons attempting to influence one side or the other to make concessions, but the positions became even more hardened. The ten-mile separation between Elkhart and Goshen seemed to be the barrier to acceptance of what had seemed a promising idea. Pannabecker's letter to his Board Executive Committee on March 22, 1956, expressed frustration:

> After working to accomplish what seemed the realization of a grand vision, it seems like defeat to concede that was not meant to be. Yet at the moment I see no way out.

Further meetings of the two Executive Committees failed to alter the situation, though both expressed deep desire for the contemplated joint program. The end of April was the low point in negotiations for the cooperative seminary work. One more consultation was to be held with possibly a final decision. It was impossible to predict what the outcome might be; the mood was one of pessimism, but a little hope was expressed in the statement that "sometime within the next few months one side or the other will take a step to clear the way." It was a prediction of faith with little substantial warrant, but it turned out to be true.

Accommodation and Understanding

The impasse was broken by a letter from Nelson Kauffman, Chairman of the Board of Education, dated May 15, 1956, which outlined a modified plan of cooperation suggested by the Executive Committee of the Mennonite Board of Education. The new plan frankly recognized the impossibility of a single location satisfactory to both institutions and proceeded to outline a new bipolar program built around two locations. It would obviously lose something in intimacy of contact but might save the cooperative endeavor. The Goshen seminary would continue on or adjacent to the Goshen College campus, while Mennonite Biblical Seminary would erect its plant and operate on the south side of Elkhart some ten miles distant.

The cooperative feature would be retained by the same exchange of faculty and by a joint library to be located on the Elkhart campus. Joint classwork was also to be provided, though the student transportation would cause some inconvenience. As a special feature there was suggested a new joint research arm to be known as the Institute of Mennonite Studies. The Institute plan envisioned facilities for expanding a program of study and witness of Anabaptist-Mennonite history and theology and its application to the present day.

President Rosenberger of the MBS Board presented the new proposed plan along with an explanatory letter to his Executive Committee and Board and awaited reactions. The first response of most members was one of questioning. Will the new plan really allow enough joint work to fulfill expectations? Will it promote closer relations in the future or solidify distinctions toward more permanent separation? Will it facilitate accreditation or make it more difficult? Will the Institute of Mennonite Studies be just a palliative for reduced cooperation otherwise or a worthwhile endeavor in itself?

Discussion with the Goshen representatives brought the conviction that this was a sincere attempt to work out a cooperative program as far as possible under the given conditions. The Goshen Seminary was ready to recognize Elkhart as the center of joint activities, the location of the joint library and the Institute of Mennonite Studies, as well as the recommended site for any other parties who might wish to join in the endeavor. It was agreed that joint classwork would be scheduled in such an amount that any student could take a minimum of one-quarter of his seminary studies in joint courses and that even beyond this there would be further exchange of professors. Concessions by the Goshen Seminary would involve them in higher financial outlay for buildings, as there would be some duplication in library and classroom space, and would give them the inconvenience of student transportation for joint work. Extra curricular activities would be separate in some cases but joint in others and faculty and student fellowship was to be encouraged.

With these qualifications the Mennonite Biblical Seminary Board was called to a special meeting June 13, 1956, to consider the revised plan. Before the final decision was made, however, a final appeal was received from President D. C. Wedel of Bethel College inviting the Seminary to locate on the Bethel campus in North Newton and giving cogent reasons for that location. The invitation was noted and read with appreciation, but the Board was too much opposed to location on a college campus and, by now, too optimistic about the new plan to seriously consider the proposal. At the same meeting favor was expressed toward the modified cooperative plan, and the Executive Committee authorized to do preparatory work on building and financing plans.

Some remaining details were hammered out and a draft of a **Memorandum of Agreement** was drawn up. The **Memorandum** carefully stated the provisions of the cooperative program and its administrative basis. Specified as an overall control body was the Joint Coordinating Committee to be composed of representatives of all bodies desiring to participate in the work. This Committee would meet annually for review and board level control. The day-by-day cooperative activities would be under a Joint

Administrative Committee representing the institutional staffs. By August the Seminary Board was ready to recommend the cooperative program to the 34th session of the General Conference meeting at Winnipeg, August 15-22, 1956.

Official Approval and Action

A little six-page pamphlet was prepared outlining the history of the discussions, the various alternatives, and particularly the proposed Plan of Cooperation with an estimate of its financial implications. At the General Conference session discussion was encouraged. Some objections were raised, even conflicting resolutions proposed, but sentiment was overwhelmingly in favor of an inter-Mennonite cooperative move, and the Plan was approved by a vote of 1,108 to 352. With the favorable Conference decision the Seminary Board met later the same day. The

MBS Board at Signing of Memo of Agreement, 1956

purchase of the Elkhart site which had previously been inspected and favored was authorized and a Building Committee and a Finance Committee were appointed. The time for action had come.

For the next two years Mennonite Biblical Seminary directed full effort to two programs, like an acrobat rider on two horses. The Chicago work continued to the end without reduction in program. Bethany was kept fully informed of all moves and the best of relations maintained. At the same time the Elkhart project demanded much time and study with important decisions at each turn. The new move was entered into with a sense of its importance. This was reflected in the report to the district conferences in 1957 in a statement that may have been slightly exaggerated but yet true:

> This tremendous project, which under God may well prove to be a most significant development in the larger Mennonite fellowship in this century, calls for earnest intercession, wide counsel, unstinting devotion, and serious stewardship, all inspired and controlled by the Holy Spirit.

Immediate responsibility for the construction of the Elkhart campus was placed upon two Board committees — a Building Committee and a Finance Committee. There was much overlapping in the membership of the two and, in fact, they had to work together very intimately.

Building Committee members were: S. F. Pannabecker, Chairman; Erland Waltner, Secretary; Elmer Baumgartner; J. N. Smucker, A. E. Kreider, A. R. Shelly; R. L. Hartzler; Olin Krehbiel.

Finance Committee members were: A. R. Shelly, Chairman; Erland Waltner, Secretary; Elmer Baumgartner; R. L. Hartzler, Olin Krehbiel, S. F. Pannabacker.

Others from the Goshen Seminary as well as other interested groups served in an advisory capacity.

One of the first tasks was to construct a tentative schedule for the completion of certain stages of the work.

The tentative dates and the dates of actual completion are shown below. In view of unforeseen difficulties it is of interest how closely the two agree.

Tentative Schedule

October 1956. Received building and financial estimates.

March 1957. Received preliminary building plans and complete publicity and financial plans.
September-October 1957. Receive completed building plans, select contractor, authorize construction.
Summer 1958. Transfer administration to Elkhart.
August 1958. Complete administration and classroom buildings.
September 1958. Open seminary work and inaugurate the new plan.

Completed Timetable

October 30, 1956. Estimates received and tentatively approved.
November 1, 1956. Legal transfer of Elkhart site property.
February 8, 1957, Preliminary plans for building, publicity, financial approved.
September 3, 1957. Plans approved and ground breaking.

July 1, 1958. Administration officially transferred to Elkhart.

September 16, 1958. Inauguration service of joint seminary operation.

Financing the New Move

The Finance Committee early adopted a five-point statement of principle, viz., (1) to emphasize the spiritual values in the program (2) to involve the entire General Conference in the effort (3) to exercise strictest economy in fund raising (4) to raise the money as needed (5) to gear the whole program through the churches. The building expenditures were to be integrated into the regular seminary operational budget and all raised together. It was estimated in September 1957, that approximately $500,000 would be necessary for building. This did not include the purchase of land, and from it could be subtracted whatever would be received for the sale of Chicago property. A four-year program was then envisaged in which $155,000 would be raised each year for combined building and operation. Actually by September 1958, the total building program had cost, including land and construction, $680,000. This was somewhat more than anticipated but the excess was covered by borrowing $240,000.

In this connection the presence of Elmer Baumgartner, President of the First Bank of Berne, on the Finance

Committee, was most crucial. His reputation and prestige with administrative officers of the St. Joseph Valley Bank in Elkhart was such that they made most unusual concessions, not only in the amount loaned, but in the terms as well. Needed funds were loaned without mortgage, at 5% interest, and repayable as able. In return strenuous efforts were made to repay at an acceptable rate and actually about $60,000 was retired each year.

In meeting construction expenses, three specific sources were helpful. The first was two unexpected large contributions. Mrs. Lucy Gilliom of Berne, Indiana, on December 19, 1956, gave to the Seminary for building purposes four hundred shares of Lincoln Life Insurance Company stock, valued at $80,000. Shortly afterward Menno Rosenberger of Pennsylvania gave five hundred and ten shares of Gillett Razor stock, valued at $20,000. These two gifts, coming so early before the real campaign had begun, were a great encouragement and spurred activity. The second source, which was anticipated, was the sale of Chicago property. This netted $157,000, not including the church building which was tentatively retained. The third was the share of building expenses contributed by Goshen College Biblical Seminary to the building for joint use. This amounted to $60,000.

The campaign among the churches was well planned. There was an initial period of information to acquaint people with the new seminary program. This was followed by more specific preparation for the financial implications and then by the more active solicitation. Church papers and mailings were the main vehicles of information but personal presentation to congregations and conferences was most productive. A. R. Shelly, who spearheaded this effort devised two major Partnership Plans. One was a Partnership Plan for churches, whereby the congregation proposed to give a specified minimum amount per year for four years. The actual number joining the Plan was not large but many more were stimulated to give, some far beyond the minimum. The Elkhart Partners Plan was an attempt to enlist individuals who would each give one thousand dollars over a four-year period. The greatest response, however, came from the multitude of church contacts. Altogether there was raised approximately $300,000 by October 1958.

The completion of construction then found the Seminary with a bank indebtedness of $240,000 and an unpaid balance on land purchase of $39,232. The liquidation of both of these in the next four years was accomplished, and November 1, 1962[1] found the last payment made.

Construction of the Elkhart Campus

The two years following the 1956 decision to relocate at Elkhart were busy years and for no one more so than the Building Committee. Duties delegated to the Committee included responsibilities to purchase the land, counsel with other interested groups, prepare a plot plan, determine the buildings to be erected, select the architect, and in con-

Groundbreaking for New Seminary Buildings

1. October 1962 Board Report, p. 28.

ASSOCIATED MENNONITE BIBLICAL SEMINARIES

PRELIMINARY PLOT PLAN

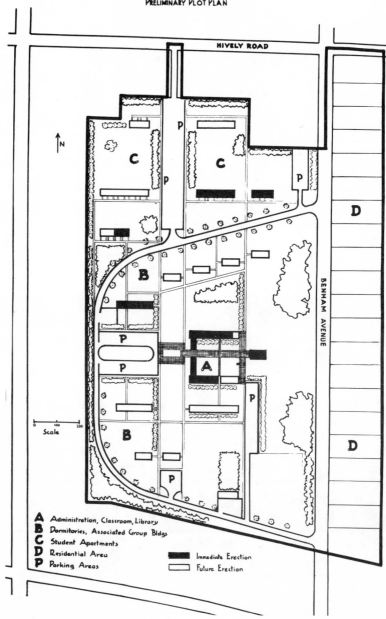

Plot Plan for AMBS Campus

sultation with him choose the type of architecture, then select a building and supervise construction. Regular progress reports to the Board were expected as well as Board approval of major decisions.

The site, already chosen, was located immediately south of the Elkhart city boundary, which at that time was Hively Avenue, and was in line with Benham Avenue which, when extended, would cut through the plot. It was purchased in two contracts, the northern part of about 32 acres from Ledger Kauffman and the southern part of about 22 acres from Walter and Wilson Everest. The total was an elongated rectangle of 54.7 acres adjoining the city by a narrow strip. The question of annexation to the city was to come up shortly and was decided in favor of annexation because of the advantages of city water, sewer, and fire protection. In view of the anticipated extension of Benham Avenue through the plot, it was decided to reserve the section to the east of Benham for residential purposes leaving about 44 acres for Seminary development. The accompanying plot plan shows the developed campus as envisaged by the architect before construction began.

September 1956 to August 1957 was the year of preparation. Such questions as the site and plot plan were worked over. Meetings of the Building Committee were held almost monthly to discuss building needs and type of construction. There was some interest in a colonial type of architecture, but anything ornate was ruled out. It was agreed that the architecture should symbolize an institution of the church, reflect an Anabaptist-Mennonite background and indicate an associated group of institutions.

The architect, Orus Eash of Fort Wayne, designed a U-shaped quadrangle complex of a simple functional nature. By September 1957, all was ready for beginning construction, and building was placed in the hands of Henry Knuck of Elkhart. Knuck had come from Holland where he had training and experience in both building and design. A third figure in the later stages was Raymond A. Werbe of the C. A. Finsterwald Company in Detroit, professional interior decorators. Werbe presented layouts for furnishings and decoration of all interiors. A fourth and key man in the overall project was Harry Martens. While serving at Bethel College, he was granted the summer of 1957 to scout possibilities for the sale of the Seminary property in Chicago. The following summer he with C. J. Dyck, then Business Manager, was able to make advantageous disposal of the Seminary Chicago assets. During the summer of 1958, and in subsequent trips from his Kansas base, Martens assisted in the Elkhart construction problems as well as in securing title to property, city annexation, tax exemption, and similar matters. He later joined the Seminary staff, becoming in 1959 Assistant to the President in financial administration and publicity.

The beginning of building operations was marked by a groundbreaking ceremony on September 3, 1958. Immediately thereafter Henry Knuck and his workmen started excavation and preparing forms for concrete work. The work had barely commenced when opposition came from Local 565 of the AFL Carpenters Union. Knuck's men were nonunion and the Local 565 Business Manager demanded that they join the AFL Union. This the men rejected and with Knuck's agreement signed up with an alternate organization, the Christian Labor Association. The move was not countenanced by the AFL Union and thus began a lengthy and at times bitter struggle. Pickets were placed at the Seminary entrances and a Chicago labor lawyer was called in to assist.

Actually the Seminary was not involved in the dispute but was very much concerned and attempted to negotiate a settlement on some reasonable basis. Others from the city joined in an attempt to influence a peaceable settlement. The climax came in a public meeting on September 28 at the Elkhart Municipal Building where it was hoped some reconciliation might be effected. The meeting was overwhelmed by a packed union group who hammered down any debate or attempt at sober comment. Martens and the Seminary attorney found no opening to take effective action. It was a baffling, frustrating defeat for those accustomed to reasonable approaches. Up to this time the Seminary had attempted to restrain Knuck from court action, but in the light of this occasion, found no alternative but to allow him to take his own course.[1] Thus began

1. Waltner's report to Building Committee Meeting, October 15, 1957, Exhibit A.

his legal battle which was not yet resolved when the Seminary buildings were completed.

Construction continued, however, in spite of pickets. Concrete was hauled in after work hours when the pickets had left, or even hauled to the entrance and then taken over by nonunion drivers. When these makeshift means were forced to cease, Knuck got his own cement mixer and hauled in materials to be mixed on the spot. He aroused a good deal of sympathy; even competititors assisted with supplies or the loan of equipment. Knuck was independent and resourceful and, though he admitted that progress was slowed, he insisted he could keep to the schedule date of completion. The pickets remained on duty for several months but eventually disappeared and the work was not molested. At no time was there any damage to property.

The little labor dispute attracted more attention and has

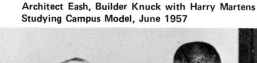

**Architect Eash, Builder Knuck with Harry Martens
Studying Campus Model, June 1957**

taken more space than it warranted. The real work of construction proceeded according to plan. Parallel with the library wing was the classroom wing and connecting the two wings, a corridor with offices and conference room including a kitchenette and storeroom. The Goshen Seminary reserved one room for faculty and dean's office and held half interest in the room for the Institute of Mennonite Studies and in the library.

The interior decoration was simplified by the extensive exposure of glass and wood. Fiberglas drapes were specified for all glass window walls facing south or west, while the walls of vertical western pine gave their own warm and interesting pattern. The wood walls were generally accepted as relaxing and pleasant, but caused one visitor to ask, "When will you erect the permanent buildings?" For furnishings use was made of the best of the Chicago tables and upholstered chairs in seminar rooms, but new equipment was installed in all offices and other classrooms.

Special mention should be made of the furnishings for the conference or board room. These were a gift of the Dunbar Furniture Company of Berne, Indiana. The items consisted of a twelve-foot conference table with sixteen matching chairs, one upholstered chair, an eight-foot sofa, two lamp tables, and a low coffee table, all of the famous Dunbar quality and of exquisite contemporary design. The whole suited well the soft old brick and wood walls.

All essential construction and installation of equipment was completed by August 1958. The new President, Erland Waltner, in his first report to the Seminary Board in October of that year called attention to the dramatic developments of the last few years and expressed indebtedness to all who participated in any way, and added:

> Especially significant in this respect are the dedicated leadership contributed by the board, the willing and faithful service of the faculty and staff, the satisfying cooperation of our students and alumni, the remarkable contribution of our architect and the building staff, the cooperative spirit manifested by others sharing in the Associated Seminaries venture, the generous gifts of the hundreds who have given financial support, and the amazing confidence of the St. Joseph Valley Bank which

is financing this large undertaking on such favorable terms. Any one of these elements is remarkable in itself, but their convergence and integration in this entire venture is surely beyond any human manipulation. This, to us, is the Lord's doing.

The Transition

The move from Chicago to Elkhart and the opening of the new program were accomplished expeditiously. The date set for the transfer was July 1, 1958. All Chicago property had been sold with possession promised by that date. The one exception was the church building which was retained temporarily by the Seminary with the understanding that for a brief experimental period the church could attempt to carry on. When this seemed to be successful, the Board of Missions took over support of the congregation and purchased the church building for that purpose. It then brought in an additional $45,000 to the Seminary for Chicago property.

The actual transfer of moveable property from Chicago to Elkhart, as well as finalizing the liquidation of real estate, was under the supervision of C. J. Dyck, then acting as Business Manager. Although much of the furniture in apartments was not moved, other things were, such as the good tables and chairs in the library and board room, some new furnishings in the reception room at 4614, the grandfather's clock, all of the pianos except one and such other things as silverware, dishes, and bedding. Especially important were the library books, both from the general library and the historical library, and all records and files and the office safe. The thirty-passenger school bus which had made daily trips from Woodlawn to Bethany was stripped of seats and loaded with boxes and books and other small items. The bus made fourteen trips with this kind of miscellaneous cargo and practically saved the price of the old vehicle. Larger furniture was hauled in three moving vans.

Little more remains to be told. This closed the "Woodlawn Story," and a new epoch begins in the chronicle of Mennonite Biblical Seminary.

5

THE ASSOCIATED MENNONITE BIBLICAL SEMINARIES

The thirteen years in Chicago have been followed by seventeen years in Elkhart to make up the thirty years which can be now celebrated. The institution is still Mennonite Biblical Seminary but is working in a new context known as the Associated Mennonite Biblical Seminaries. The development in these seventeen years has been remarkable, and the difference between "then" and "now" is notable, though the two are not essentially different in spirit. Then, in 1958, there was a full-time staff of nine with six part-time assistants; now, in 1975, there is a full-time staff of fifteen with only three part-time. Then, there was a simple, barely sufficient quadrangle of library, offices, and classrooms; now, there is also a beautiful chapel with fellowship hall, a student lounge, more office space, and a pleasant landscaped setting. Recently added to all this is the new library facility. Then, the cooperating seminaries had but a hesitant approach to joint classwork — a kind of fringe benefit; now, there is complete integration of curriculum, faculty, and student body. Perhaps most significant of all, then, the two institutions were separated geographically by eleven miles and socially by differing interests and barriers of unknown and untried relationships; now, the two seminaries are united on a single campus with seventeen years of experience together and a common understanding of the task and its approach. It is not an organizational merger of institutions nor a complete amalgamation of all aspects of life, but it is an integration of purposes and of effort in a common task. What has been continuous through the years has been the Anabaptist-

Mennonite consciousness of discipleship and the desire to grow in the leading of the Holy Spirit. It is the result of this leading that is occasion for celebration. What was then a hope has now become a reality and what lies ahead remains to be seen. These developments do not come suddenly, but are matters of growth. While growth is slow and hardly noticeable from day to day, there are, as in human life, outstanding events that mark the culmination of development and the beginning of a new era. Two such events characterize the seventeen years from 1958 to 1975. The first was the selection and inauguration of a joint dean for the two seminaries in 1964; the second was the relocation of the Goshen seminary on the Elkhart campus in 1969. Both of these gather up other developments that contribute to a new quality of life and provide a springboard for the future. It will be convenient then to look at the ripening relations of the joint life in three periods, which might be designated as: Beginning Association, 1958-1964; Building of a Common Life, 1964-1969; and Integration of Program, 1969-1975.

A. Beginning Association, 1958-1964

Opening

Three special events marked the opening days of the first year together. On Tuesday, September 16, the first day devoted to joint classes, there was a solemn and formal inauguration of the associated work. President Waltner presided, while all those present stood in the reading room of the new library. Dean H. S. Bender spoke of the importance of this occasion. Other administrators emphasized this, and the two student body presidents led in prayer seeking the blessing of God on the new venture. On September 28 occurred the dedication of the new buildings. Dr. Walter Roberts, then President of the American Association of Theological Schools, was the speaker. He likened Mennonite Biblical Seminary to a family that had lived for a number of years with uncles and aunts and had now moved into its new home. He called for a fellowship in commitment, worship, and understanding the gospel. The third occasion for celebration was the inauguration of Dr.

Dedication Service for the New Campus, September 28, 1958

Erland Waltner as President of Mennonite Biblical Seminary on October 26. It was held in the nearby Church of the Brethren and opened with a colorful procession of representatives from fourteen other seminaries. Arthur S. Rosenberger, Chairman of the Seminary Board, gave the charge and spoke of God's leading in the past and the responsibilities of a leader in this new associated relationship. He voiced the hope that not only these two but other groups of the Mennonite brotherhood might be led to enter the association.

First Year

With this memorable beginning the first year in the new association was under way. The MBS staff was essentially that of Chicago. All members had been invited to move and all had accepted except Don Smucker who had previously resigned. His relationship was not entirely terminated, however, as he continued for a year as a special lecturer in Christian Ethics. In administration the President was assisted by Harry Martens part-time for a year and thereafter on a regular full-time basis for a decade. C. J. Dyck served temporarily as Business Manager from his Chicago residence where he was still engaged in graduate studies, while Estelle Bartel, later Mrs. Herman Enns, tended the day-to-day

Newly Constructed Campus viewed from East showing Tent for Dedication Service and the Lone Elm Tree later deceased

office work. S. F. Pannabecker agreed to continue temporarily as Dean, while A. R. Shelly and Magdalen Friesen continued their respective tasks in Public Relations and Library. Frieda Claassen continued as office secretary. The teaching faculty was rather limited with only three full-time members — J. J. Enz and Marvin Dirks in their former fields and William Klassen added in New Testament. These were supplemented by part-time help from Leland and Bertha Harder and from nearby experienced pastor-teachers, A. E. Kreider and J. N. Smucker.

As to students, with one or two exceptions, the Chicago group all transferred to Elkhart. With new additions, enrolment reached a total of 58 for the year. It should be added, however, that 24 of these were auditors or part-time students, mostly wives. All three years of the B.D. program were well represented. The number of women students was gratifying; eight were full-time students in the M.R.E. curriculum, four being members of the newly organized group of Women in Church Vocations.

The curriculum of the new institution varied little from that of preceding years. To accommodate to the Goshen program, Greek and Hebrew language requirements were introduced; a change from the quarter system to the semester system modified some courses. In general there was somewhat greater emphasis on Bible and correspondingly less in other areas. A joint curriculum study was inaugurated but no change resulted.

Cooperative Work

It was the possibility of cooperative work that had most aroused interest, and here there were three primary areas in the Associated Seminaries program — the joint classes, the joint library, and the Institute of Mennonite Studies. In the joint class work each seminary profited by the resources of the other. The Goshen men who taught courses open to Elkhart students made an impressive addition to the teaching faculty. They included Howard Charles, John H. Yoder, Lawrence Burkholder, Paul M. Miller, and H. S. Bender. The courses specified as joint offerings numbered seven, totaling fifteen hours, in the first semester; and eight, totaling eighteen hours, in the second. Students from both institutions took advantage of these courses, and there was a hearty enrolment of from eleven to twenty-five in each of them. The student response to joint work was encouraging.

The joint library involved three collections — the main collection at Elkhart, the core reference collection at Goshen, and the Mennonite Historical Library also at Goshen. Additions were made to all; the largest number went to the main library, with reserve and reference books in small number to the Goshen Library. All collections were available to all students and a shuttle service provided reasonably prompt service for books from the different locations.

The Institute of Mennonite Studies under C. J. Dyck as Director and H. S. Bender as Assistant Director made some progress during the first year but was limited by Dyck's operating on fringe time under the pressure of graduate studies. Nevertheless, important steps were taken in the organizing of an Advisory Council which first met in January 1959, and the planning of research projects. One of these was an Anabaptist Bibliography to be done by Hans Hillerbrand and the other a study of Christian responsibility in social concerns by John H. Yoder. It was also decided to hold an Anabaptist Seminar in June, the first such IMS study. Though a small beginning, these presaged the many worthwhile projects to be undertaken in succeeding years.

Joint Faculty and Student Body, Fall 1958

The joint faculty met several times during the first year. One meeting was devoted to a serious study of the meaning of a "Biblical Seminary"; others were concerned with the curriculum study. The first jointly sponsored special lecture series was delivered March 5-6, 1959, by Dr. Eugene A. Nida of the American Bible Society, speaking in four lectures on "Communicating the Gospel." The Joint Administrative Committee had been active all through 1957 and was composed of Presidents Mininger and Waltner and Deans Bender and Pannabacker. They met about a dozen times during the 1958-59 year for discussion and decision-making on such joint concerns as budgets of the IMS and joint libraries, joint course offerings, joint faculty and student meetings, the AMBS annual lecturers, the school calendar and the proposed summer session.

While the list of joint activities is quite extensive, apart from the joint classes and joint faculty meetings there was little evidence of intimate contact either between students or faculty members of the two schools. Joint classes were held on two afternoons each week. Other afternoons and the mornings were devoted to separate classes. Chapel services, which were in the morning, were also separate and no attempt was made to make them joint. The fall and spring MBS retreats, following the former pattern, were Elkhart affairs, as were the Seminary Women's Fellowship meetings, and the Baccalaureate and Commencement services. The Cooperative Bookstore, carried over from Chicago, was an Elkhart enterprise. Toward the close of the year, in May, Goshen students and faculty were invited by the Elkhart group to a social afternoon at Pierre Moran Park. The occasion was enjoyable and came to be repeated in following years at the invitation of either seminary. The appetite for this exchange increased, and in the second year Goshen students and faculty joined in the annual spring retreat in May. It was a foretaste of many such closer exchanges to come.

There was a deeper sense of independence and academic responsibility at Elkhart than had been possible in the Chicago affiliated pattern. Spiritual growth was fostered through daily chapel services, a weekly prayer service in large or small groups, and attention to personal relations. The Spiritual Life Committee was a six-member group of four faculty and two student representatives. A Seminary council with faculty, staff, and student members dealt with matters concerning the whole seminary family, while a Seminary Student Organization and a Women's Association were concerned with student and family affairs.

Progress

On the whole the first year was satisfying and was reported as successful with good promise for the future. It was a beginning, of course, and the next five years brought many advances as faculty and students of both institutions became adjusted to each other. In the matter of faculty and staff there were two phases to the growth. The first was in training; four members of the faculty had been teaching while finishing graduate study. In 1962 it could be announced that all had received their doctorates – J. J. Enz, C. J. Dyck, William Klassen, and Leland Harder. This freed them for more wholehearted attention to teaching and gave the school a better status. Then, secondly, there were additions made to the faculty – Clarence Bauman in

Theology and Orlando Schmidt in Music and Worship. Several new courses broadened offerings in New Testament, Theology, Worship and Pastoral Care. On the staff Marlyn Fast was added in the Business Office, Ray Hacker in the Library and Loris Habegger in Church Relations.

In regard to joint course offerings, the philosophy had never been clarified. In the first year the courses to be offered jointly were selected more or less at random, though required courses were avoided. The next year others were added and, in the third year, it was agreed to include Christian Education, specialized courses where only a few enroled, and certain required courses, such as Christianity in America. By 1964 joint courses were offered in every department and approximately one-half of the offerings were joint courses. Every full-time student was involved. To make the expanded joint program more convenient two full days were devoted to this work, with all classes at Goshen one day and all at Elkhart the other day.

The student participation in increasing joint class work is shown graphically in the following table. The number of "student-hours" given is the product of the number of students taking joint class work by the number of hours of joint work for which they registered.

Participation in Joint Classes

Year	Autumn Semester	Spring Semester
1958-59	234 student hours	278 student hours
1959-60	227	287
1960-61	277	404
1961-62	442	549
1962-63	348	561
1963-64	499	726

The last figure illustrates how the force of circumstances built up registration in joint courses, for in the semester two faculty members were on leave and all Bible offerings were in the joint program.

The Joint Dean

The question of a Joint Dean had been in the minds of some of the Elkhart staff in view of S. F. Pannabecker's temporary assignment and its review year by year after moving to Elkhart. This question suddenly came to the fore with the death of Dean H. S. Bender. Bender had tendered his resignation, but was still serving in the fall of 1962. At the opening of the school year on September 17, he spoke to a joint convocation which packed the Goshen chapel. His subject was "Perspectives of the Joint Program." He was inspired by the prospect before him, and to quote from President Waltner's report to the October 1962, Board meeting:

> In a striking blend of retrospect and prospect he spoke with deep feeling of how the associated program had significantly strengthened the work of each cooperating institution and of how significant is the role of the associated program in the further development of inter-Mennonite cooperation on many fronts.

His moving address became practically his last words, for he passed away four days later. His contribution to the whole movement had been most crucial — encouraging, directing at every step, and occasionally applying a cautious brake. His support was unquestionable and wholehearted. His place as dean was temporarily supplied, but the problem of a permanent Goshen dean became more insistent.

The suggestion of a common dean was immediately put forth. The Goshen situation was different than that at Elkhart due to the Goshen Seminary's connection with the College. H. S. Bender had been administrative head of the Seminary while Paul Mininger, as President of the College, participated in matters of overall concern. In Elkhart the dean was in charge of the academic program only and the President was the administrative head. Besides this difficulty in coordinating the two jobs, the question was raised as to how far the constituencies were ready to follow in the close identification which a joint dean might suggest. Discussions raised other knotty questions also, such as who should select him, to whom would he be responsible, and what should be the scope of his authority.

The matter had almost been dropped, but then Dr. Walter Roberts of the Association of Theological Schools on a visit suggested that the dean, as such, be responsible

90

for the academic affairs of both institutions and other responsibilities be considered separately. From this came an interesting solution to the problem. The new dean was to be a "Shared Dean." The Goshen Board of Overseers in January 1964, appointed Ross T. Bender as Dean with the understanding that Mennonite Biblical Seminary might also name him as dean if they wished. His primary responsibility, involving perhaps two-thirds of his time, would be to the larger task at Goshen while otherwise he would also serve at Elkhart — really a man with two hats. This was a little less than the previous hope of a joint dean but acceptable as a reasonable compromise. Bender assumed his double responsibility in the fall of 1964 with an office at each location. In reviewing the appointment after a year of operation and in succeeding discussions of the deanship little is heard of a Shared Dean and the office became real joint dean.

Accreditation

Before leaving this five-year period, three other developments must be mentioned. The most outstanding was the receiving of accreditation by the Association of Theological Schools (ATS). This had been desired in Chicago, but the Mennonite program was so tied in with the Bethany operation that it was impossible to extricate a separate institution. At Elkhart the case was different, and after a year of operation, the ATS was ready to recognize Mennonite Biblical Seminary as an associate member. This challenge to press forward was given encouragement by the accreditation of the Goshen Seminary already received in 1958. More strenuous efforts were given to reaching standards in faculty, finance, library and curriculum. The desired accreditation was announced in June 1964. It had been preceded by an informal advisory visit, the study and filling out of extensive schedules and an official on-campus inspection. The favorable consideration provided, as the President reported to the Board, "human assurance concerning the validity and soundness of our building of a program of theological education." While there was further growth required and rising standards to be met, this successful effort, more than anything else, marked the end of the beginning years.

Conference Relations

A second important decision concerned the relation of the Seminary to the General Conference. The 1940 Board reorganization had made the Seminary Board subject to General Conference election and hence responsible to the Conference. The Conference, while backing the institution, took no financial responsibility for it. For support the Seminary went directly to congregations and individuals for contributions. Since, unlike the colleges, Seminary tuition receipts were negligible, about 80% of the Seminary operating budget and all construction expenses had to be secured by current gifts. There was a certain freedom in this and a consequent stimulus to cultivate good church relations. The advantages were offset by the uncertainty of income. Some congregations and districts could be depended upon to respond to need, but nevertheless the Seminary was forced to operate on a month by month basis. The preliminary study for accreditation had revealed a critical view of the "intangible conference support."

Repeated discussion of the problem led the Seminary Board in their March 1963, meeting to request the General Conference to consider making the Seminary Board an additional Conference board parallel with the four other boards and providing a subsidy of not less than $2,000 per month to be included in the Conference budget. The Conference had already appointed a committee to study the relationship and the basic assumption of Conference responsibility was clarified and affirmed. A December 1963, action of the General Conference Executive Committee provided that thereafter the Seminary would be promoted as part of the General Conference budget, though the Seminary would continue its own promotion also, and that the Seminary would share in undesignated gifts which were to be proportioned among the recognized boards.[1] The new arrangement gave proper focus to the place of the Seminary in the total mission of the Conference, and helped to stabilize support. At a later date the Seminary was also granted representation on the General Board.

1. *The Bulletin, Mennonite Biblical Seminary,* January, 1964, summarizes the development in an article, "The Seminary and the General Conference."

Students and the Ministry

A third development in this first period was really the beginning of a new attitude toward the ministry. It was disconcerting at first but had positive value. Students had been among the most ardent promoters of the Seminary. They had expressed satisfaction and support of the efforts to establish a creditable training institution at every step. They had felt free to criticize at times and their comments on seminary experience were accepted with appreciation. They had been active in cultivating joint activities — forums, retreats, socials — and in sponsoring college student conferences on church vocations. They had raised a scholarship fund to support a black exchange student from Atlanta. Now, students seemed to be questioning the traditional forms of church life and the ministry. An increasing number were taking one year only of seminary work and not continuing in a B.D. program. Seven out of fifteen dropped out of the middle class in 1963. The year 1963-64 saw a series of Wednesday morning student forums devoted to a wide range of stimulating topics questioning the traditional forms of church life and work and personal vocational decisions, but including also the ethical implications and mandates of a Christ-centered faith. Some hesitated to prepare for the overly esteemed status of clergy as they saw it. They were looking for "new and creative forms of the ministry."

Not only students but Seminary faculty and Board were drawn into discussions hinging on this same approach. What, they asked, is the Seminary's responsibility toward nonpastoral and nonmissionary students, those with other church vocations as teachers, journalists, graduate students? And what about non-Mennonite students? Increasing interest was shown in biblical and theological training for the laity and for professional people. This is referred to in the President's report to the Board in October 1964, as one of the "persisting problems" of the Seminary. It reached the Joint Coordinating Committee of the Associated Seminaries, and the same year they approved a consultation on broadening the range of seminary offerings with special consideration of nonpastoral students. Essentially it would mean expanding a ministerial training school into a theological school.

Actually the Seminary had always welcomed all sincere seekers, but up to this time few besides those planning church vocations had applied. It would be up to the new dean in the succeeding years to determine policy and procedures to meet a new challenge.

The period of Associated Seminaries' beginning may be somewhat arbitrarily regarded as closing with 1964. A useable physical plant had been built with a creditable faculty, reasonably assured financial backing, an accredited program, and a smooth working organization with a centralized academic administration. This, with some of the persistent problems, was the contribution to a new cycle of building.

B. Building a Common Life, 1964-1969

The Chapel

There was one building project in the original plan which had never been completed. That was the chapel. Plans for it were proposed in the Six-Year Plan of the Development Committee in 1962. As the financial picture cleared, preliminary plans were approved in October 1963, and Architect Charles Edward Stade, famous for the chapel at Valparaiso University, was chosen for the designing. Several preliminary sessions were spent with the architect in an attempt to interpret Anabaptist-Mennonite ideals in the building. Construction was begun in the summer of 1964 and completed for dedication in June 1965. The chapel turned out to be an unusual structure, commanding the campus with its rugged simplicity and inner integrity — beautiful without a show of beauty and practical in every arrangement. Along with the chapel was added an extension to the classroom wing which allowed for a student lounge, long needed, and other service rooms. About the same time occurred the erection of a duplex of apartments for larger families, a maintenance building, and landscaping of the quadrangle area. This practically completed the campus development and provided adequate physical facilities for the growing program as envisaged at that time. The planning and financing were by the Elkhart Seminary though Goshen men were invited to share in the deliberations. The whole operation signaled an unmistakable commitment to

Chapel Under Construction, 1964

Volunteer Workers headed by Sam Ediger (third from right)
who worked on Chapel Construction

the Elkhart location and the Associated program.

This round of construction cannot be passed by without noting the unusual voluntary service of skilled builders and other workmen. Sam Ediger, as building superintendent, with Olin J. Schmidt and Jerald Stucky, all of Kansas, contributed approximately one year of time; John R. Dyck of Rosthern, Saskatchewan, spent six months on the job. Others could be mentioned who served for shorter periods; some of these were students. Of the latter, outstanding was Willard Stucky in beginning construction and handcrafting the pulpit furniture.

The brochure prepared for the Dedication Service lists the major volunteers and adds that "nearly one hundred others contributed their labors of love." Some of them traveled a distance of 2,000 miles. It was estimated that the contribution of these workmen would approximate in dollars one-third of the cost of the project, while the craftsmanship was judged as excellent by qualified inspectors and visitors. Procurement of the organ, which was part of the original plan, was postponed for a time but was realized in 1969 through specially designated funds.

Along with the campus development came a changing neighborhood. As the bean field had become a seminary campus, so a larger open area to the north was occupied by a shopping center, a Nazarene church and eventually three filling stations. To the east was a mammoth complex of apartments and a city water development with a high tank, and to the south two churches, Lutheran and Methodist, and an expanding residential development. A Negro, Mr. Fred Carter, applied for the purchase of a Seminary lot for building in 1964. Quite an uproar ensued among some of the white neighbors, including burning of a cross, but the seminary was committed to "open occupancy" and completed the sale after holding a neighborhood consultation. Mr. Carter's house turned out to be a credit to the community and his lawn the best kept on the street. A second black family moved in later without opposition.

Inner Development

For determining the Seminary's inner development the two most influential factors were the receiving of accreditation and the appointment of a common dean. Accreditation opened the door to opportunities not available otherwise and implied a more responsible participation in movements occurring in the wider field of American seminary education. C. J. Dyck in 1965 was the first to take advantage of an ATS Faculty Fellowship grant available to accredited members for further study; Clarence Bauman received a similar grant in 1967, as did others later. Also selected graduates of five years standing became eligible for fellowships for Continuing Theological Education under the Parish Ministers Fellowship Program. The first to take advantage of this was Leonard Wiebe who spent a year at Union Theological Seminary in 1969-70. Harold Regier followed the next year with a semester at Mennonite Biblical Seminary with the same fellowship. Others also in following years.

The President attended a 1965 Conference on Continuing Education sponsored by the ATS and North Central Association of Colleges, and the Dean attended a Consultation on Degree Nomenclature. The Seminary became a member of the Accredited Theological Schools of Ohio and Indiana (ATSOI), an organization devoted to securing tax-reducing contributions for theological schools from industrial and commercial businesses in the area. The first year some $3,000 was received. The most satisfying financial benefit resulting from accreditation, however, was participation in the Library Development Fund. The joint library had profited by the Goshen Seminary's previous membership; now for two more years (1964-66) MBS could receive up to $3,000 in matching funds for increased library expenditures. From this came a great boost to the growing library.

More significant in the internal development of the Associated Seminaries was the effect of installing a joint dean. It showed up immediately in the curriculum and cooperative relations. The policy of separate courses seemed out of date. Duplication was discouraged, and the number of joint courses doubled the first year, jumping from twenty-three in 1963-64 to forty-three in 1964-65. In 1966 four days of the week were devoted to joint work and separate classes almost disappeared. In 1967-68 no distinction was presumed between joint and separate courses and in effect all work was on a joint basis. Chapel services also were joint four days per week. In addition to the joint academic work was the distribution of student counseling responsibilities among faculty members and the joint planning on faculty development. Incidentally a direct telephone connection — a smaller version of the "hot line" — was installed between the Dean's two offices. What had previously been the MBS Fall Lectures became a joint AMBS lectureship. In 1965 also occurred the first joint deputation group of twenty men, nine from Goshen and eleven from Elkhart, who traveled to churches, both General Conference and Mennonite (MC), in Illinois, Missouri, and Kansas. It was in this flush of common activities that the Joint Coordinating Committee in the October 1965, meeting raised the question, "Why the great increase in joint offerings?" After discussion, it was noted that "we could not close our eyes to the pressure created by our joint progress towards a single campus and/or a single seminary." It seemed all reports were favorable, and any earlier fears were dispelled.

Students and Life Style

During these years, 1964-1969, there was continued concern over student issues. First, enrolment was disappointing. From an overall full-time registration of around fifty the number decreased to as low as thirty-five in 1968-69. Moreover, as noted before, many of these were one-year students and failed to finish a ministerial course. Graduates in the B.D. program were reduced from ten or twelve to six or eight. Criticism was voiced at the shortage of ministers produced by the seminary. To remedy this the churches were urged to stimulate more volunteers and a recruitment program under a new Admissions Counselor, David Habegger, was introduced in 1967 with some positive results.

Apart from numbers there was expressed dissatisfaction over the life style of some students. College and popular styles were carried into seminary where beards and jeans and sweat shirts had been unknown. Incidents of carelessness were observed and overt expressions of independence. There was something of a confrontation between pastors attending a renewal seminar in 1968 and students. Echoes of this got back to the churches with consequent criticism.

From the Seminary side a Task Force on Life Style, composed of faculty and students, was brought into action to work over the problem without resort to rigid, legalistic control.

Much of the student independent thinking was not destructive but arose from criticism of the church and the ministry as too complacent toward social issues, war and race particularly. A vocal minority raised objection to the newly installed organ in 1969, protesting the expense in a time or rampant poverty, the display of elegance instead of humility and the lack of spiritual quality in church music. This was not traditional Mennonite opposition to musical instruments but concern for a living church in contemporary society. The Board was sympathetic and even offered to remove the instrument if there would be some unanimity in the Seminary community that it was harmful. This never happened and little further was heard of the matter, but the incident illustrates a type of serious thinking current among students. The problem over life style was perhaps as much a product of the generation gap as of distorted ideals. It was reported by 1970 that there seemed to be a new spirit moving among the whole Seminary community. Bible study, faculty prayer meetings, Koinonia groups, and organ vesper services brought a renewed closeness and understanding.

The year 1969-70 stands out as a kind of landmark in many unrelated ways. It was the year graduates chose to celebrate commencement without the traditional caps and gowns and without the commencement procession; it was the first graduating class to have a member with a full bushy beard; it was the first class to have a woman graduate with the full three-year ministerial degree; it was the first time that the two graduating classes had joint services for baccalaureate and commencement. These services were also preceded by the first joint commissioning service. It was the end of the sixties and the beginning of the seventies.

Integrated Campus

Without question the outstanding event of these years was the relocation of the Goshen-based seminary on the Elkhart campus and the consequent merging of activities that became possible. The move had long been foreseen as obvious if the two institutions were to make the most of a cooperative endeavor. The marked increase of joint interests had pressured the move. It came in a clear-cut decision in April 1969, that Goshen College Biblical Seminary would separate itself from Goshen College, becoming simply Goshen Biblical Seminary. It would be placed under its own Board of Overseers with its own administrative officers and its own financial program, and move to the Elkhart campus. The MBS Board had already expressed an official welcome and offered to transfer possession to a joint ownership on any mutually satisfactory basis. Visible evidence of the change occurred in the summer of 1969 when the Goshen Seminary Library with card catalog, files, and miscellaneous materials was moved into the Elkhart main library. The enormous task of relocating books and integrating cards was accomplished and the whole Associated Seminaries collection of 55,000 books, not including the Historical Library, was available in one place. Faculty also were reassigned, allowing office space for the Goshen faculty members in Elkhart rooms. The move not only provided better library service but made possible a stronger community life which became a significant new emphasis in the Associated Seminaries program.

Dean's Seminar

The major effort to provide an adequate theological basis for contemporary ministerial training occurred during the years 1967 and 1968 and was known as the Dean's Seminar. It came about in the context of disturbing movements in theological education. The ATS biennial meeting in 1966 challenged seminaries to justify their existence in an ecumenical era. Unless a seminary had a particular significant contribution to make, its survival was hardly warranted. In fact some seminaries were closing and others were merging to meet the new stringent financial crises. The ATS was proposing a policy of "Clustering" whereby seminaries should be grouped in university or other centers and there pool their resources for improved theological education and financial economy.

The proposed policy was threatening to those schools with a conscious denominational basis, a small enrolment

100

and an isolated location, but the logic was inescapable. For the Associated Seminaries it meant a deep probing of purpose and procedure. It raised the question of relocation, with a choice between an urban, university area or a group of congenial denominational institutions. Before taking any action it was necessary to thoroughly study the place of a seminary of the Anabaptist-Mennonite tradition in its own church context and in its ecumenical world setting. This was the purpose of the Dean's Seminar.

Dean Ross T. Bender was of the conviction that there was a distinctive and unique contribution to be made to theological education from the Free Church tradition, and that this contribution was not adequately recognized in the major ministerial educational stream. He proposed a study of this subject. The Joint Administrative Committee approved and applied to the Lilly Endowment, Inc., for a grant toward its implementation. The Lilly Endowment was impressed and allowed a generous $60,000 for the two years' project. This enabled Dean Bender to give full time to this study and others to assist and to make useful world-wide exploration of emerging churches. Eventually the results were published in a volume, *The People of God* (Herald Press, Scottdale, Pa., 1971). While Bender spearheaded the study, there were associated with him six members of the AMBS faculty — C. J. Dyck, Leland Harder, William Klassen, Millard Lind, J. C. Wenger, and John H. Yoder. They met in over seventy sessions in the two-year period seeking to answer such questions as: What is the distinctive Free Church vision? At what points does it vary from contemporary options? How can it be translated into a program of theological education? Following this was the attempt to develop a model for ministerial training in this tradition.

Without attempting to summarize the prolonged discussions, it can be noted that the proposed model postulated certain requisites for the curriculum. Theological learning, the study insisted, takes place in the context of **Christian community** and of **personal commitment**. Further, it takes place through **participation in a pilgrimage**, through **scattering in different geographical and cultural locations**, and through the **pursuit of a diversity of professional goals** absorbed in a ministering church.

These conclusions were not immediately embodied in a new curriculum, but they became the guiding principles by which certain aspects of the former educational enterprise were enlarged upon and certain new aspects introduced. They gave direction and stability to the Associated Seminaries program for the following years.

The decade of the sixties closed with mixed satisfaction and dissatisfaction in the current situation. Disappointing was the measure of student unrest and lack of precision in purpose. Nonministerial students exceeded in number those anticipating the pastoral ministry. The economy caused apprehension. There was uncertainty in wider theological circles. On the other hand, deeply gratifying was the integration of the new centralized program, the developed physical facilities, an enlarged and experienced faculty, and especially the new assurance in purpose and procedure as a result of the Dean's Seminar.

C. The Seminary in the Seventies, 1970-75

This is the third period in the life of the Associated Seminaries, and we are now speaking in the present tense. Have we two seminaries or one? The answer is officially and legally two, but in spirit and operation, one. Faculty, students and physical plant are indistinguishable; administration, financial support and constituency have clearer distinction. The two seminaries are accredited separately, both by the Association of Theological Schools and by the North Central Association of Colleges and Secondary Schools, but with the presupposition of associated operation. There was a time when accreditation of the associated program as a single operation was proposed. It was studied by the two seminaries, encouraged by Association of Theological Schools, and finally approved in principle by the two boards but for practical reasons not effected. The whole work is essentially an integrated program, the latest evidence being the issue of a single catalog for the joint operation.

The sixties have left their mark. What was student unrest has quieted down to an accepted revolution in freedom of dress, the use of contemporary music, an emphasis on gifts of the Holy Spirit, the "House Church" and a greater participation of students in seminary administration. Student representatives are involved in every active committee, sit in on faculty meetings and board meetings, and are consulted on such things as senior examinations and curriculum.

Student interest in the ministry has not decreased but has shifted position. The pastoral ministry is regarded as one form of several possible ministries. Yet those preparing for the pastorate about equal in number those interested in other forms. The registration by categories in the latest Associated Mennonite Biblical Seminaries Catalog for 1974-76 shows the following alignment, M.Div. being the pastoral category.

	M. Div.	M.R.E.	M.A.R.	1 Yr. Theol.	Unclassified	Total
GBS Men	27	6	7	6	8	54
Women	1	3	0	4	5	13
Total	28	9	7	10	13	67
MBS Men	19	4	3	3	5	34
Women	0	4	2	2	2	10
Total	19	8	5	5	7	44
Overall	47	17	12	15	20	111

MBS Graduating Class of 1974
left to right: Andrew Lu, Bruno Epp, Virgil Gerber, D. Ernie Penner, Dale Suderman, Richard Friesen, Richard Bucher, Robert Dalke

Not counting the Unclassified, who would be distributed variously, the forty-seven pastoral candidates compare well with the forty-four others.

If there is an uplift in the outlook, it may be due in part to the country-wide change toward a more relaxed student atmosphere, but it must also be credited to a new emphasis and new program on the part of the seminary — a program promoting spiritual life and the many opportunities in the ministry. There has been some revision of courses and the addition of offerings in Peace, Anthropology, and Transcultural studies, but the real difference is a change in the approach to method.

Emphasis on Experience in Learning

The Dean's Seminar emphasized personal experience and community participation as the vehicle of learning. This shows up most clearly in the department of the Work of the Church and especially in its practical field work. New experience-based learning opportunities have been introduced, of which the most important might be:

Experience in Christian Community
Supervised Experience in Ministry
Congregationally Supervised Pastoral Education
Clinical Pastoral Education

Experience in Christian Community was a new program introduced in 1968 as central to the new model then being evolved. It took over the responsibilities of the former Spiritual Life Committee and sought, by more intimate contact and personal response, to deepen sensitivity to mutual accountability. It gathered up the forum discussions, chapel services, cell groups (K- or Koinonia-groups), commissioning service, and extended into many forms of field work. It nourished personal relationships between students and faculty members and created understanding and an undergirding Christian fellowship.

Supervised Experience in Ministry took the student outside the seminary community to serve in one of several areas such as preaching, counseling, Christian education, or youth work in an actual congregational setting. It was introduced in 1970 as part of an overall clinical approach to the practical field. Keyed into this was adequate supervision by experienced faculty and a regular evaluation by peer-group members undergoing the same experience. A special case of the above was the Congregationally Supervised Pastoral Education. Six students were sent out in the fall of 1969 to serve for one year in four selected congregations, chosen for the availability of responsible local supervision and nearby institutional counseling opportunity. It was an intensive and enlightening experience. In the spring term they returned along with their supervisors for an evaluation period. They manifested enthusiasm and reported a new vision of the possibilities for the pastoral ministry. Other students were encouraged to follow the same program and it became a continuing program providing an opportunity to test out the pastoral assignment. Some who had been indecisive were attracted by this new challenge to the congregational ministry.

Clinical Pastoral Education is another specialized form of experience in an approved institution under professional supervision. Closest home is the newly organized St. Joseph Valley Clinical Pastoral Education Center opened in 1972. It is administered by Oaklawn Psychiatric Center with the participation of Notre Dame University School of Theology and the Associated Mennonite Seminaries. This and other clinical centers approved by the Association of Clinical Pastoral Education provided opportunities for experience in a wide range of ministries in hospital, home, or congregation.

These are some of the means by which seminary training is oriented around learning through experience. Other aspects of the same might be mentioned, such as the encouragement given students to take a year at some other theological institution or to engage in an off-campus transcultural experience such as summer in the Urban Ministries Program for Seminarians in Chicago.

Transcultural Experience

Somewhat similar to these forms of learning through experience, but organized differently and with a transcultural bent, are two new programs: The Overseas Mission

Training Center and the Theological Center. The Overseas Mission Training Center is an integral part of the expanding seminary work but involves also two participating mission boards — the Elkhart Mennonite (MC) Board of Missions and the General Conference Commission on Overseas Mission. The Director, Robert L. Ramseyer, is responsible to all three bodies. Ramseyer, who was serving at the time in Japan, returned in the spring semester of 1971 to open the program and then in 1972 began long-term service. Students or candidates sponsored by one of the participating bodies are accepted and a special schedule of studies designed for each individual. This may involve seminary studies or training and experience elsewhere. A part of this program is provision for mission and cultural studies in the seminary curriculum.

The Theological Center is related to transcultural experience and ministerial experience and is an effort to bring to the campus capable churchmen and women of different backgrounds for a period of residence. It may be for a month or several days with a few lectures but more time for personal interviews. The first of these, in October 1969, as Churchman in Residence, was Takashi Yamada of Japan, an effective pastor and energetic promoter of evangelism through small groups. He was followed by Dr. Marthe Ropp, French Mennonite physician working in Java, experienced in healing through the medical profession but convinced also of the spiritual resources for healing. They have been succeeded by experienced pastors, missionaries, and theologians.

Through these various forms of guided experience, a deeper concern for the work of the church has been aroused. With the renewed interest in the pastoral ministry there has continued also the desire for theological training on the part of many who do not feel the call to that vocation. This has been encouraged, and besides the long-standing curriculum for a master's degree in Christian Education, a course of study has been designed leading to a master's degree in Peace Education or in a broader field of Religion. Others seeking personal orientation in theological studies or in lay church ministries are welcome to a one-year theological course in which wide liberty is given to choose relevant subjects of interest. To this one-year of study have been attracted men and women whose professional life is devoted to chemistry, biology, medicine, the law, or teaching. These too are an asset to the lay ministry of the local church, and at times have even been attracted to the ministry as a profession.

Attainment of Seminary Goals

The question that may properly be asked at this stage is whether in these seventeen years the Seminary has attained to a reasonable degree the goals projected in the move to Elkhart. Probably everyone closely involved in the movement would agree that they have. The one most disappointing factor in the 1958 relocation was that it was impossible to agree on a common location and two cooperating units had to function across a ten-mile chasm with its implications for intimacy. That has been bridged much sooner than was then thought possible. Dean H. S. Bender expressed himself at the time to the effect that getting together would be quite possible, but it would be twenty years down the line. Actually it only took ten. This has been the greatest factor in facilitating other lines of co-operation — common faculty relations, a united student body, similar ideals in life style and spiritual development. The common location and the common dean have done much to promote satisfactory curriculum development and to provide proper supervision of student field work.

As to why the Associated Seminaries experience turned out as well as it did, there might be various explanations. It was obviously an idea whose time had come. Other promising inter-Mennonite moves were indicating a growing spirit of cooperation, and the common struggle against economic pressure and social problems underlined the need for a common approach. This generally favorable atmosphere, however, would not have been sufficient without more concrete factors. The men involved in the negotiations were fortunately, or providentially, well suited for their delicate role. They were thoroughly convinced that the move was desirable, not only so but that unless this attempt succeeded, the whole cause of inter-Mennonite relations would be set back. They sought sincerely to understand each other and encouraged confidence to the point that minor differences could be discussed and cleared. The same spirit of mutual trust and determination to succeed characterized the Joint Administrative Committee as it took over and extended to board members and faculty. Students early recognized the common interests and pressed for success in the move. Even the early doubters were willing to wait and be shown and eventually rejoice in the outcome.

Faculty

One of the principal advantages of the associated work and especially of the integration on one campus was the enlarged faculty. Both institutions at the time of accreditation had a faculty barely meeting the minimum requirements. The MBS faculty in 1964 presented six full-time teaching members supplemented by part-time assistance from two administrative officers and one half-time teacher. The GBS faculty was similar with five full-time teaching faculty and part-time assistance from five others. All departments are now adequately staffed with sufficient resources to allow a more relaxed teaching schedule and to cover absences for sabbatical leaves. Team teaching and other innovations also have become possible. The faculty line-up for 1974-75, which is representative, shows the following:

Teaching Field	MBS	GBS	Others who have served MBS in Former Years
Bible — O. T.	J. J. Enz	Millard Lind	
Bible — N. T.	Erland Waltner+	Howard Charles	Wm. Klassen, 1958-64, 66-69
	Gertrude Roten*		Archie Penner, 1964-66
	David Schroeder(1)		A. E. Kreider, 1958-62
History & Theology	C. J. Dyck	J. C. Wenger	
	Clarence Bauman	John H. Yoder	
Church & Ministry	Leland Harder	Paul Miller	Walter Gering, 1960-64*
			J. N. Smucker, 1958-62*
Christian Education	Bertha Harder*	Ross T. Bender+	
		Weyburn Groff+	
Missions & World Church	R. L. Ramseyer		S. F. Pannabecker, 1958-67*
Music and Worship	Orlando Schmidt		M. J. Dirks, 1958-61

Note: +Administrators with part-time teaching
*Faculty members serving part-time only
(1)Serving one year, on leave from Canadian Mennonite Bible College

Besides these, GBS has had much assistance from members of the Goshen College faculty and both seminaries have profited from staff members of Oaklawn Psychiatric Center. On occasion well-qualified professors from other institutions have been brought in for a term or semester: Dr. J. A. Oosterbaan of the Mennonite Seminary and University of Amsterdam in 1968, Dr. Josephine Massingberd Ford of Notre Dame University School of Theology in 1971, and Dr. Ed P. Blair of Garrett Theological Seminary in 1972-73.

Student Enrolment

Student attendance has been referred to as one of the persisting problems. At one time it was thought that an enrolment of fifty would be a reasonable figure to attain. It would be ample to provide a stimulating community and sufficient to produce replacements for the church's ministry and its expansion. That number of ministerial students has never been reached. Further, the changing concept of the ministry has reduced the number even more. The accompanying graph of attendance shows a higher enrolment of men — at one time nearly fifty — in the early sixties and again in the early seventies. In the intervening years the number was below forty. What this presages for the future remains to be seen.

What is clear from the enrolment figures, and on the accompanying graph, is that total enrolment has improved in recent years. The larger total, however, comes from the increasing number of women taking seminary work and the large number of men taking studies in preparation for church service other than the pastoral ministry. Some of these will doubtless, with experience, feel that the pastoral ministry after all is the best outlet for their interest. Much has been attempted in recent years to promote appreciation for the pastoral possibilities with some positive results, but a greater recruitment effort is still needed. Several women have graduated now with full professional training for the pastoral ministry; others in growing number are pursuing related lines of study. The church must be ready with more open arms to accept their ministry either as individuals or in a ministerial team.

Mennonite Biblical Seminary

Graph of Enrolment Data by Years and Categories

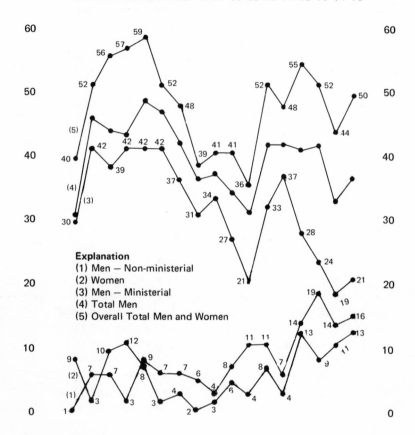

| 1958- | 59- | 60- | 61- | 62- | 63- | 64- | 65- | 66- | 67- | 68- | 69- | 70- | 71- | 72- | 73- | 74- |
| 59 | 60 | 61 | 62 | 63 | 64 | 65 | 66 | 67 | 68 | 69 | 70 | 71 | 72 | 73 | 74 | 75 |

Explanation
(1) Men — Non-ministerial
(2) Women
(3) Men — Ministerial
(4) Total Men
(5) Overall Total Men and Women

Observations

Sharp changes from one year to the next, e.g., 1970-71, are not as significant as the general nature of the curve.

Rather obvious is a swelling enrolment of both men and women in the early 60's (1959-63) and the early 70's (1969-72). Obvious also is the general decline in the later 60's, especially 1965-68.

The minister enrolment, Line (3), shows a general decline except for the years 1969-71 when the large increase roughly balances the excessive decline in the two previous years.

The general increase of non-ministerial men, Line (1), is of interest.

The enrolment of women, Line (2), shows a temporary rise in the early 60's (1960-62) followed by decline and a slow general increase thereafter.

It is worth noting that the 1974-75 figure for Women (13) includes two who are registered in the M.Div. program and could be added to the "Ministerial" number.

110

Institute of Mennonite Studies

The Institute of Mennonite Studies has turned out to be a valuable asset to seminary research and has promoted wider inter-Mennonite involvement than any other regular feature of the program. C. J. Dyck has been the Director through the years with assistance earlier of H. S. Bender and more recently of John H. Yoder and a number of others. There is an Executive Council of eight and a group of thirty IMS Associates. The Executive Council is autonomous in effect but dependent on AMBS administrative decisions in personnel and budgeting. The Institute has been concerned with Anabaptist studies and current Mennonite concerns including missions, peace, social and political questions. An imposing list of some thirty research projects has been undertaken and seventeen of them completed with ten published monographs.

AMBS Faculty as of 1974
left to right (standing): D. Schroder, C. Bauman, P. Miller, V. Claassen,
C. J. Dyck, J. Enz, L. Harder, O. Schmidt, R. Ramseyer, G. Roten, M. Lind,
P. Roten, J. C. Wenger, H. Charles
left to right (seated): R. Bender, E. Waltner, J. Hertzler, M. Miller,
B. Harder, D. Schumm

Wider Mennonite Association

The one point at which early hopes have not been realized is the participation of other Mennonite groups in this ministerial training endeavor. In the planning years, 1956 and 1957, representatives from the Mennonite Brethren, The Evangelical Mennonite Church, the Brethren in Christ, and the Evangelical Mennonite Brethren were invited to the consultations. Some response was found with occasional attendance on a personal, rather than official, basis. None finally chose to participate in the move and subsequently Mennonite seminaries were established by the Mennonite Brethren at Fresno, California, and the Eastern Mennonite College at Harrisonburg, Virginia. The Brethren in Christ did officially approve three seminaries for their ministerial students, one of which was the Elkhart Associated Seminaries. On the other hand, in 1965 a Council of Mennonite Seminaries was organized which included, with the Associated Mennonite Biblical Seminaries, the two mentioned above and the Mennonite Brethren Bible College at Winnipeg. Through this Council much of the value of the associated work is being recovered. All joined in sponsoring two Institutes of World Evangelism, one in 1967 and again in 1968; a faculty consultation was held in 1968.

In concluding the account of this period of growth together, we can well remind ourselves of the many ways that much progress was made in this joint effort at preparing personnel for the various church ministries. As pointed out by President Waltner in a review of "Ten Years of Experience in Cooperation" for the Joint Coordinating Committee in 1968, we have learned much. What was true then is even more true now, six years later.

We have learned that it is possible for two Mennonite groups to work together.

We have learned that the needs and problems in our respective church constituencies are more similar than they are different.

We have learned that the issue of Mennonite identity is

of considerable significance for the entire Mennonite brotherhood.

We have learned that what goes on in the Associated Seminaries has significance far beyond our brotherhood ... in larger theological discussions, in scholarly meetings, in church ministries, in other denominations.

We have learned that there are serious limitations in being small and genuine advantages in working together.

We have learned that the problem of the image of the minister or pastor is a crucial one for seminaries.

We have learned that seminary education is a demanding and expensive undertaking — in personnel, in finances, in moral and spiritual support of the churches — probably greater than most realized or than many are even now aware.[1]

Thirty years is hardly enough to pass judgment on an endeavor like this in seminary education. Mennonite Biblical Seminary has already doubled the lifetime of either Witmarsum or Wadsworth. It is tied to the Church itself, which under God's guidance looks forward and calls for ministering servants qualified for whatever future the Church is destined to have.

RETROSPECT AND PROSPECT

Mennonite Biblical Seminary is celebrating its thirtieth anniversary in 1975. It would be well to recall that it is fifty years since Witmarsum Theological Seminary was in its best years and that this year is now the sixtieth anniversary of the opening of its predecessor in 1915. For that matter it is one hundred years since the predecessor of all, the Wadsworth Institute, was in its last good year with thirty-one students enroled. And again it is the one hundred and tenth anniversary of the erection of the Wadsworth Insti-

---

1. Somewhat abbreviated from *The Bulletin,* Mennonite Biblical Seminary, Jan. 1969, p. 7.

tute building in 1865. There is much to celebrate in 1975, whether thirty years, fifty years, sixty, or one hundred or even one hundred and ten years.

The accumulation of these dates suggests that training for the ministry is not an isolated event but a continuing concern of the church. Each of these days suggests changing conditions and new demands. The ministry has never been a static matter; it has ever faced new prospects and persistent problems. This is good; it is God's way to growth. The greatest enemy to growth is contentment with traditions tied to the past, not the uncertain future with its challenges to change.

The Mennonite ministry started as a "counseling service" — encouragment to fellow-believers under persecution in Reformation days. It adopted preaching also as a means to admonition and instruction. It was even attracted at times to the ceremonial and sacramental institutions of church life. But it has ever been the attention to a heartfelt commitment and disciplined life that has ruled the Mennonite church concept and its ministerial service. Today sees a growing return to the emphasis on this personal interrelation of believers under the guidance of the Holy Spirit. Preaching and church administration are in vain without it.

A story from one hundred years ago illustrates the need then, even as now.[1] A traveler to the Palatinate visited the old Pastor Stauffer at Ibersheim. The venerable pastor was troubled by changing conditions — loss of the old simplicity, youth marrying outside of the church, members scattering, new preachers with education. The visitor asked, "Friend Stauffer, how did you come to preach, have you studied?" The old pastor replied:

> I'll tell you. My first sermon I suffered so I thought I would despair, but it went better later. When my turn comes I take a sermon from a collection, read it, see what the man says, pray God to give me something in the heart too, then write out the theme and remarks of what I will preach. I take this to the pulpit to direct thoughts. There is good preaching only when one experi-

---

1. From the *Mennonitische Blaetter*, XXIX, (Sept., 1882) p. 69.

ences the truth in his heart, then it has entrance to
listeners.

What stands out here is the old pastor's despair in
meeting the new situation, but also his triumph in realizing
that there is the possibility to bridge all gaps with honest
underanding. God's truth is eternal.

Conditions may change, demands on the church and its
members may change, the form of the ministry and the
preparation of pastors may change, but the Holy Spirit
continues to work through committed believers with understanding hearts. The seminary attempts to build on this
foundation an intelligent discernment of the needs of the
day and a preparation in the resources of the gospel to
meet those needs.

AMBS CONSULTATION SPONSORED BY THE JOINT COORDINATING COMMITTEE, November 18-19, 1968, a ten-year review of the AMBS experience and possibilities for the future. Participants represented the Mennonite Brethren Church, the Evangelical Mennonite Church (Canada), the Evangelical Mennonite Church (USA), the United Missionary Church and Missionary Church Association, as well as the Goshen College Board of Overseers, the Mennonite Board of Education Executive, the Mennonite Biblical Seminary Board of Trustees, and AMBS faculties and students.

AMBS Choir

SAMUEL FLOYD AND SYLVIA PANNABECKER have invested their lives deeply in educational and missionary services of the General Conference Mennonite Church. A graduate of Bluffton College (1917) and of Witmarsum Theological Seminary (1918), "S. F." began a teaching/administrative role which continued throughout much of his life, first as instructor at Bluffton College (1918-23). Called to missionary service in China, the Pannabeckers served there in various capacities between 1923-41, except for 1933-34 when S. F. was Acting Dean of Bluffton College. During 1944-46, he served as MCC Relief Commissioner to China. Having completed his Doctor of Philosophy degree at Yale in 1944, he came to his administration/ teaching role at Mennonite Biblical Seminary to serve as Dean (1946-48), as President (1948-58), again as Dean (1958-64), and as Registrar (1964-69). His strategic place in the development of Mennonite Biblical Seminary in Chicago and its relocation and development at Elkhart, as well as his historical research and writing gifts, qualify him eminently as the author of "The MBS Story." Without the insightful and faithful partnership of Sylvia, his distinguished career would not have been the same.